BREAK
THE
LAW

A Story of a Reimagined
Legal Career and a
RECLAIMED LIFE

BREAK
THE
LAW

JOHN R. KORMANIK, ESQ.

To every lawyer who picks up this book:
You do hard things every damn day. You ought
to have the life you not only want, but deserve.

Contents

Acknowledgments

Have you ever done something you believed impossible?

Writing this book has been that, for me. This book has truly been a team effort. It has taken a team to whom I owe a debt of gratitude which, it feels as I write these words, I will never be able to fully repay.

First and most importantly, I thank Michelle and Allie who possess more patience than you can imagine and an unwavering belief in me. Michelle, thank you for picking me up when I fall, for calling me on my BS, and for empowering me to be all I can possibly be as a husband, father, coach, and human being. Allie, your ceaseless belief in the power of human connection, your patience with me when I fall short of expectations, and your power to show me the way through your words and actions has put me on the path to be the person I want to be.

I am immensely grateful to my mentor, the Honorable Darrel Perry, who taught me more about being an attorney and person than everyone except my mother, Barbara.

A special thank you goes to my editors, whose keen eyes, thoughtful suggestions, and passion for allowing my voice to shine through these pages have made this book all it could possibly be. Working with you has made me a better writer, author, and person. I also want to thank my design team for bringing the vision for this book to life with such creativity and passion.

To all my friends, both old and new, who supported me through this process (even though you didn't know you were doing so), your support and friendship mean the world to me.

Finally, to every single lawyer, both those I've met and those who I haven't, thank you for doing the work you do, no matter the area of law you've chosen to practice in. You inspire and motivate me each and every day. This book is dedicated to you.

Introduction

"Next to the ministry I know of no more noble profession than the law."

~ WILLIAM JENNINGS BRYAN

I agree. The law is a noble profession. And yet . . .

The law as an industry is broken. Don't believe me? I've got the receipts. In survey after survey, lawyers tell the world what we in the profession already know: being a lawyer is hard, being a good lawyer is harder, and being a great lawyer is harder still. Couple that challenge with holding onto your humanity and reaching your full potential as a human being—in the workplace, the home, and the community—and it can seem like an impossible ask.

The landmark 2016 Hazelden Betty Ford Foundation ABA study revealed that approximately 33 percent of the more than twelve thousand practicing attorneys surveyed qualified as problem drinkers, 28 percent struggled with some level of depression, 19 percent experienced anxiety, and 23 percent experienced a significant level of stress.[1] The authors of the study concluded:

---

[1] Patrick R. Krill, Ryan Johnson, Linda Albert, "The Prevalence of Substance Use and Other Mental Health Concerns Among American Attorneys," *Journal of Addiction Medicine* 10, no. 1 (January/February 2016): 46–52, https://doi.org/10.1097/ADM .0000000000000182.

"Attorneys experience problematic drinking that is hazardous, harmful, or otherwise consistent with alcohol use disorders at a higher rate than other professional populations. Mental health distress is also significant."[2]

Despite the awareness of these grim statistics, the picture is not improving. For example, a survey conducted in 2022 reported startling percentages of anxiety, depression, and isolation among lawyers, clocking in at 67 percent, 35 percent, and 44 percent, respectively.[3] It seems that despite all of the focus, hand-wringing, and authentic concern, things simply are not improving for the lives of attorneys across the United States and, presumably, around the world.

There is a saying I learned on how to become a great trial lawyer: when a juror speaks, believe what they are saying. The same holds true here. You have to believe what the lawyers are saying; they're telling the truth.

As a lawyer who practiced for over two decades in both the public and private sectors, I have come to know these issues well, either firsthand or through my relationships with close friends and colleagues. I wanted to do something about it, and this driving principle ultimately resulted in my leaving the active practice of law and becoming a Certified Professional Coach.

I did not leave the active practice of law because I was stressed out, depressed, or done with being an attorney. I loved the law and being a lawyer; I still do. I loved owning my law firm and being entrepreneurial; I still do. In other words, I didn't leave because I was burnt out. I left because I figured it out. I knew I could empower lawyers like no one else if I turned to focus my

---

2 Krill, Johnson, Albert, 52.
3 Debra Cassens Weiss, "About One-Fifth of Lawyers and Staffers Considered Suicide at Some Point in Their Careers, New Survey Says," *ABAJournal*, May 10, 2022, https://www.abajournal.com/news/article/19-of-surveyed-lawyers-and-staffers-said-they-considered-suicide-at-some-point-in-careers.

attention on attorneys, enabling them to escape those horrible statistics.

I am confident that one underlying cause of the depressing reality shown by survey after survey of attorneys is the recognition by individual attorneys that they are not living up to their full potential—the recognition that, in fact, they aren't even coming close. I'm also convinced a contributing factor is living a suboptimal existence in one or more areas of their lives. Finally, I believe many lawyers have forgotten who they are as people.

I know the law can be reclaimed as a truly noble profession again if, and only if, attorneys in the system take control of their lives. Not by looking outward for some magic potion, gimmick, platform, ploy, or hack, but by looking inward to identify who they want to be and why, so they can do the work necessary to achieve that state.

You may ask, "Why are you writing *this* book?" That's an excellent question with both a simple and a more nuanced answer. Let's begin with the "simple." I decided to write this book because I have grown tired, I mean bone-tired, of hearing other lawyers say things like, "I'd never allow my kid to go to law school," or "If a friend asked me if their kid should go to law school, I'd be a hard NO," or "I wish I'd never gone to law school." I was tired of being out in the world and witnessing great attorneys hesitate, even for a beat, to tell a stranger what it is they did for a living because they were somehow embarrassed about their chosen profession. I was tired of seeing attorneys conflate their identity with their work, thinking who they were could be summed up with "I'm a lawyer," when in fact practicing law is not, really, who anyone *is*, but instead their profession, the thing they practice so they can achieve their goals and vision for their life. Finally, I was tired of—and even frightened by—seeing lawyers who, at the age of fifty, or sixty, or seventy, or even eighty, would say something like, "I don't know what happened. I started practicing law and never looked up in time to decide what I wanted."

I've written this book because lawyers are noble *and* lost. Attorneys will be served by this tale if they not only learn the lessons that follow, but *act* on that knowledge—which, of course, is the hardest part.

The longer answer to why I wrote this book is, as I said, a bit more nuanced and requires a brief departure to look at my own career. I did not come to be an attorney as a logical or inevitable next step in my life, like many do. I had another profession before going to law school, serving others as a Registered Respiratory Therapist during the years around 1984 to 1995, in New Jersey, New York, and San Diego. Through this time of my life, I understand the immense pressure health care workers can experience, as I worked while the AIDS crisis was in full bloom and also in a busy Level I trauma center caring for the critically injured. When I decided to go to law school, I was making a big leap. I was thirty-five, married, owned a home (with a substantial mortgage—a product, if I'm being honest, of trying to keep up with the Joneses), was the father of a two-year-old, owned a dog . . . you get the picture. But I *really* wanted it. When I shared my desire to change careers with my wife, Michelle, she simply said, "Don't mess it up, John."

I did not mess it up. Instead, I bested my goal of finishing in the top 10 percent of my law school class and graduated magna cum laude (fifth in my class). I also proceeded to take the real-world experience I had gained up to that point and began mentoring, "coaching" if you will, my younger and less experienced classmates. The law was much more than a "job" for me; it was, indeed, a calling in that season of my life. A full life requires personal evolution and my personal growth continued.

Now I am called to serve those who serve others, my family in the bar. One way of doing so to reach as many as possible with maximum impact was to pen what follows. I've invested significant time, effort, and, honestly, a few tears, in the writing of the book you hold in your hands, and if I can impact just one of you, the ripples flowing from that—one lawyer who has reclaimed their life—will, in fact, dent the universe. I will have achieved my goal of reclaiming the law as a noble profession.

The best way I know to share all I've learned is through story, and so what you are about to read is a tale of two lawyers, Jefferson "Jeff" Simpson and Amy Thorngood. The attorneys and the law firms they run are fictitious. Although you may identify with some of the things Jeff is experiencing, any resemblance to an actual lawyer or law firm is purely coincidental. But I hope the truths contained in this fable make an actual impact on your life.

It is time to break the law, reach your full potential, and learn the ways to optimize your life. If you agree, or are even the least bit curious, read on.

Chapter 1

Jeff

"We cannot change anything until we accept it.
Condemnation does not liberate, it oppresses."

~ CARL JUNG

Fuck.

Jefferson "Jeff" Simpson, the new managing partner at Goldsmith, Harper, & Broadhurst, APC, drives down Interstate 5 in a midnight silver metallic Tesla Model X toward his office in downtown San Diego.

He shakes his head as he passes the Encinitas Boulevard exit. He should be exiting there to go to his morning Masters swim at the YMCA's 50-meter pool. He loves his swims, not only for the physical benefits, but for the competition and community too. Today, though—like many days—there's no time. "I'll figure my shit out and get back to it . . . one day," he mutters to himself.

Traffic is light at this hour; it only takes him about thirty minutes to arrive at the firm. Jeff turns on the lights to his office overlooking San Diego Bay and the Coronado Bay Bridge. It is 0645 hours. (Having worked in health care prior to law school, Jeff never lost the habit of using military time.) He is, of course, the first one at the office.

He puts his travel coffee cup on the corner of his standing desk and connects his laptop to the three-screen monitor array sitting before him. When the screens light up, he pulls up his calendar on the left, his electronic to-do list on the right, and his email on the middle. He takes a deep breath and glances at the calendar for the day. It's going to be another busy one filled with meetings, administrative tasks and, of course, legal work. He also notices his daughter's varsity basketball game this evening at 1900 hours. *I hope I make it this time.*

He sighs audibly, takes a sip of his coffee, and glances out the window into the lightening sky.

Next, he reviews his to-do list, and after thinking there's no way he'll get everything he wants done, done, he turns to his email. The number of unread messages disgusts him and causes a knot to form in his stomach. When he shut his laptop down at 2330 hours last night, he could swear he had caught up. How in the hell did so many accumulate overnight?

"Shit," he mutters.

He sighs and begins to plow in.

There's a knock on the door. Pam, Jeff's longtime legal assistant, pops her head in. "Good morning, boss! Do you need anything for your 8:30 meeting?"

Jeff looks over the center computer monitor. Pam doesn't arrive at work until 0815 hours. *I've been in my email for how long?* he thinks. *How the hell did that happen?* He came in early to get some things off his desk and somehow had frittered the time away, lost in email. "I think I'm good, Pam. Thank you," he says with a cheeriness he doesn't really feel. He finishes with the final few emails, gathers his things, and walks to the main conference room for his first of many meetings today.

The conference room, named "Nazaré," the town in Portugal where adventurous surfers ride some of the biggest waves in the world, is a beautiful space, with a wall of glass and a large boat-shaped mahogany table in the middle of the room. On the right-hand wall is a surfboard print by world renowned surf and landscape photographer Aaron Chang. Everyone who comes to GH&B and is lucky enough to be in the Nazaré room has commented that the view from the room is *the* most stunning in all of downtown San Diego. Jeff is oblivious to all these things as he robotically walks into the room, puts his laptop down in front of his typical seat in the middle of the table, facing away from the windows, and grabs his second cup of coffee for the day from the credenza under the surfboard.

This first meeting with the practice group leaders is essential. In attendance are the heads of various practice groups: Andrew, head of the tax group; Jasmine, head of the real estate group; Robert, head of the litigation group; and Sophie, head of the trusts and estates group. As the team sits around the table, Robert is the first to speak. "Jeff, we *need* to hire a few more associates. The litigation group is drowning! We're turning down great work because we don't have the bandwidth."

Not to be outdone, Jasmine piggybacks on Robert's plea: "Robert, most of your litigation is 'one-and-done'; the real estate group has a significant amount, I'd say 65 percent, of repeat business. Our clients aren't happy with how long things are taking and, frankly, the delays are almost all on our end and due to lack of proper staffing. We don't have sufficient support staff and so the attorneys are doing work they most definitely did not go to law school to do."

Jeff can feel his mind begin to spin.

After this initial volley of what Jeff thinks of as "woe is me" complaints, the team gets down to business. They go over case counts and statuses, revenue generation, marketing and sales activities, and team needs. The meeting lasts ninety minutes, and at the conclusion, Jeff is worn out. He wonders how he'll continue to maintain his focus for the next meeting, which is about to begin. Pam has, at times, tried to build space into his calendar between meetings for Jeff to decompress and clear his mind, but he generally asks her not to. He can't see the value in even a five-minute buffer, which to him feels like wasting time.

Meeting number two is the firm's monthly business meeting, where the heads of the practice groups, who remain in the room, are joined by Ruth, the firm's COO, Jonathan, the chief human resources officer, and Susan, the VP of finance. After everyone is seated, Susan shares the fact that accounts receivable are up. Jonathan speaks about the increasing associate turnover rate and how tight the hiring market is at the moment.

As Jeff listens and feels the weight of their words, he doubts his abilities, not as an attorney, but as a CEO, and thinks, *I don't know if I'm the right person to be the managing partner of this firm. Shit, I don't know if I'm the right person to be the managing partner of any firm! What am I doing here? Do I have the skill set?*

The meeting wraps up fifteen minutes late, at noon. As everyone is filing out, Ruth pulls Jeff aside. "Are you okay? You look exceptionally tired today."

For some reason Jeff finds it hard to look Ruth in the eye. "I'm fine. A bit tired and, frankly, overwhelmed this morning."

"I get it," Ruth says. "Being managing partner of this place must feel like being . . . oh, I don't even know if I could put it into words!"

"Thanks, Ruth," he says. "I do appreciate it, and I appreciate you. The thing is, they don't teach you how to be a managing partner of a law firm of GH&B's size in law school! As a matter of fact, law school teaches you nothing about how to have a successful law practice or the business of law. As much as I tried to observe Zoe when she ran this place, none of it prepared me for when she retired and I took the reins. Plus, she made it look so damn easy! I feel like I need an MBA to run this place."

"Remember, though, you have a team here to support you. You do not have to take all of the weight of the entire firm on your shoulders." Ruth gives him a smile before walking away. Her words were kind, but did nothing to ease Jeff's mind.

Especially considering he's already completely behind for the day. He's already been at work for five-and-a-half hours, but he hasn't done a bit of real legal work. *At my hourly rate of $975 per hour,* he thinks, *that's over $5,000 of unbillable time today . . . so far!* His whole day has been spent in his email responding to other people's priorities and in two meetings—which he knows are important to the health of the firm, but don't help him get through the lengthy to-do list for his practice that awaits him.

As Jeff walks down the hallway, he overhears two associates speaking. He recognizes their voices—it's Bart and Connie. Both have been with the firm for about four years as lawyers; before that, they clerked at the firm during law school.

"I'm not sure I'm cut out for this type of firm," Bart says. "Besides you, Connie, I don't really feel connected to anyone here even though we're now back in the office 75 percent of the time. It is certainly better than the COVID times, but . . ."

"I know what you mean!" Connie replies. "That and the stress of the work is beginning to get to me. It's even affecting my relationship with my girlfriend," she laments. "Marie asked me the other day: 'Is it really worth it? Why don't you work for yourself?' I had no answer for her."

"Well, yeah. I think over 60 percent of lawyers work for themselves or in small law firms. This place may be too big for us," Bart concludes.

Jeff arrives back in his office and thinks about the conversation he's overheard. He can't get over the fact of how different this "new" generation of lawyers is from his. Connection? When he was an associate, he wasn't concerned about "connection"! He was focused on making his billable hour requirement and ensuring he was of value to the firm so he could make partner. If he made friends or was "connected" with some of his coworkers, great, but that was not a priority. When years ago, he had performed a DiSC personality assessment, it confirmed what he already knew—he was an extremely high "D," which meant, and still means, he's fast paced and task oriented, at times to the detriment of the people around him who have a different DiSC makeup.

He thinks of the older generation of lawyers at the firm, those who came up before him, and how they speak with a sort of glee about how hard they worked. How it was a "win at all costs" game, which pitted associate against associate, partner against partner. As they tell it, they had to walk a mile uphill to and from school in the snow with no shoes to get ahead in their industry. They were tough and think his own generation of lawyers is soft. He wondered what they'd make of Bart and Connie's complaints.

Jeff again thinks about how easy Zoe made managing the firm look. She appeared to be a master juggler who had no trouble keeping all the personalities, business demands, and legal work balanced effortlessly in the air. *Managing a law firm with three distinct generations of attorneys, not to mention staff, is a challenge,* he thinks to himself. *And honestly, I don't know if I'm cut out for it.* He realizes this is the second time today he's questioning his ability, which has become typical for him, he concludes.

By the time Jeff snaps out of this unproductive inner meeting with himself, the clock reads 1300 hours. He looks at his to-do-list and decides it's time to tackle the sticky legal issues. Instead, though, Jeff spends the next stretch of time picking some small, relatively unimportant things off his list, responding to the seemingly endless stream of emails demanding his attention, and taking phone calls from clients and opposing counsel in his cases.

Most things he checks off his list are things Walt, his paralegal, could easily do for him, but Jeff isn't good at delegating certain work to Walt. He's not sure why that's the case. Plus, Jeff feels good getting some things crossed off the list in between the emails and phone calls. He *feels* productive; God knows he is *busy*.

As he works, one thing, a much heavier lift, still looms. Jeff must review what is hopefully the final draft of a massive motion for summary judgment and other documents he's filing on behalf of one of GH&B's long-standing and most important corporate clients. Although this client has stellar in-house counsel, it has been coming to the firm for its litigation matters for decades. Finally, at 1400 hours, Jeff is getting down to the work he ought to have started this morning when he first arrived at the office.

As he opens the electronic folder housing the documents, there's a knock on the doorframe. (Jeff always works with his door open.) He sees it's one of the firm's star associates, Melanie, who's been with the firm for about five years. *How in the world has it been that long?* he thinks.

"Hey, Jeff, got a sec?" she asks. "I want to run something by you."

"Of course Mel, come on in and grab a chair." With this, Jeff moves from behind his desk to the sitting area in his office. The "spaceship" that is Jeff's computer monitor array makes it impossible to stay behind his desk and have a meaningful conversation with anyone. Also, Jeff despises having a desk between him and whoever he is speaking with. It feels so disconnected. Which apparently matters to him a little too.

"What's up?" he asks.

Melanie proceeds to dive into a sticky trust litigation question.

Although Sophie, the practice area leader, is probably the lawyer best suited to the intricacies of the question, Jeff lets her continue. He believes she likely has the answer to her question already and is wanting to verbally walk through her thought process to become comfortable with her conclusion. Jeff has often offered to help Melanie in any way he could, and he meant it. This seems to be one of those times. And so he sits and listens, outwardly calm, his mind half on Melanie and half thinking of the damn MSJ he should be working on.

Jeff asks some pointed questions to help her refine her legal analysis, and as he had predicted, she had the solution to her question all along. As they wrap up their conversation, Melanie snorts and acknowledges as much. "I guess I needed to process what was going on in my head! Thank you so much. I hope I didn't interrupt you too badly."

"No, no, of course not! You know I have an open-door policy and I mean it when I offer to help. We're a team, so, when you succeed, we all succeed. Keep up the great work!" he says.

It is now 1435 hours.

Jeff repositions himself at his desk and begins reviewing the extensive summary judgment pleadings. *Okay, time to finally do some of the work I went to law school, and incurred all that student loan debt, to do.*

The pleadings are extensive: motion, memorandum in support, ten affidavits. All told, the documents he's reviewing would fill at least one box, perhaps two, in the old days. *Thank goodness I don't have to look at these things on paper!*

Jeff is about one-third of the way through his review when Pam buzzes him. "Jeff, Mr. Schindle is on the line. I know you're trying to get that MSJ done and dusted—the filing deadline is tomorrow—but he says it's urgent."

Jeff takes a deep breath, audibly exhaling. "Go ahead, put him through."

Josh Schindle is a new client with the firm with the potential for significant ongoing work for the real estate group. This is important to GH&B's bottom line, especially as their real estate group has been struggling with client creation and messaging as they compete against boutique law firms who specialize in real estate and larger firms with bigger names and massive street cred. Landing Schindle and his company was quite a coup for GH&B, and Jeff played a big part in that.

"Josh, Jeff here. What can I do for you?"

"I need to talk with you about the little lady who's in charge of your real estate shop, what's her name . . . Jasmine, and her team . . ."

The conversation with Schindle is chock-full of misogynistic and racial undertones that Jeff pushes back on, a bit, but not as much as he'd like. By the time he ends the call, he is seriously wondering if Josh's business is worth the trouble.

Pam knocks and peaks her head into Jeff's office. "Sorry about that, he was so insistent." She looks down at the floor.

"What is it, Pam?"

"Oh, I know having 'difficult' clients is part of the deal, but he's *so* challenging," Pam laments.

"I know what you mean."

"Anyway, I wanted to see if you needed anything before I leave for the day."

Jeff looks at the digital clock on his desk in shock. It reads 1800 hours. *How the hell did that happen?* he thinks. "No, thanks, Pam. I promise I'll have those documents ready to be electronically filed by noon tomorrow."

Pam knows Jeff is a man of his word and he'll do what he says, come hell or high water. She turns to leave, "Doesn't Emma have a basketball game tonight? I saw it on your calendar."

"Yes, she does, but I've *got* to get this review done. She'll understand." As he speaks, Jeff feels a pit in his stomach. *Will she?* He recalls a long-ago conversation with a law school classmate after first semester exams.

Jeff is transported back in time. The classmate, Ben, seemingly had it all. Among the well-off in law school, Ben was weller-off than most. He came from a well-to-do family and both his parents were well-respected litigators. Shoot, his dad, Ben Sr., represented some heavy hitters in some big Department of Justice investigation into executive branch wrongdoing. As a 1L, Brad was driving around in what was for the time a nice BMW.

Jeff, Ben, and a few other classmates had gone to the pub after their last final to blow off some steam. After a few beers, the conversation inevitably turned away from the stress and strain of finals to more human conversation. Someone mentioned how good Ben had it, with the nice car and famous parents. Ben's retort now rang out in Jeff's head and his gut: "You know what, I'd trade all of it to have had my father show up at one fucking high school soccer match when I played." Ben's face had been serious, as he took another gulp of his Guinness.

The scene played out in Jeff's head in nanoseconds. "I'll explain it to her tonight when I get home. She's a smart kid, she gets it."

"Of course she does," Pam says, trying her best to sound sincere.

"Good night, Pam."

"Night, Jeff."

Pam turns to leave and begins to close Jeff's door.

"You can leave it open," he says.

Her face grows serious. "Jeff, you're *too* available sometimes. Not now. You're already missing your daughter's game for goodness' sake. The least you could do is focus and get that summary judgment done. I don't want to be working late tomorrow!" She takes a beat before continuing. "I remember back in the day when we had to have everything to the courthouse by 4:55 p.m. for filing to make the deadline. Remember those days, Jeff?" She smiles. "Now, with e-filing, you lawyers think you have until 11:59 p.m. and you often take every darn minute up until then! But I don't want to be here until midnight tomorrow night because you didn't get your stuff done."

For the first time today, Jeff laughs. "Okay, okay. You can shut the door. Honestly, I don't know why I don't do that more often when I've got a project like this due."

Pam smiles and closes the door. Unbeknownst to Jeff, she puts a large Post-it Note on the door, which reads "DO NOT DISTURB, DEEP WORK IN PROGRESS." Pam also drew a rough skull and crossbones on the note.

"Fuck," Jeff says as he audibly exhales, and returns to the thing he had planned on immersing himself in almost twelve hours before.

A few hours later, Jeff turns the lights out in his office overlooking the bay. It is 2130 hours.

He's not quite done with the pleadings, but they'll be manageable tomorrow and he should be able to keep his promise to have them to Pam by 11:00 for filing by noon. "Hope springs eternal," Jeff mutters. He can do some further work on this when he gets home, along with continuing to wade through emails and, hopefully, getting to bed at a reasonable hour tonight.

He takes the elevator down and walks out the front doors of his building. As he walks to his space on the parking deck, he wonders if it is all worth it. This car. The nice house in the hills of Leucadia overlooking Batiquitos Lagoon with the, honestly, ungodly monthly mortgage. The private school tuition for Emma, a senior at The Bishop's School. The golf club membership. All of the trappings of a high-powered attorney with a perfect life. All the desirable things everyone out there believes are tangible signs of "success." All the things that leave him feeling trapped.

During his drive up the 5 Jeff wonders if his wife, Jen, would understand if he chucked it all, quit his law practice at GH&B, and became a yoga instructor or something. He smiles. She's always fully supported him, but that ask might be too much.

He and Jen have been married for twenty-five years. They've had their struggles, as any couple married for a quarter decade has, and remain deeply in love. But the stress and strain of Jeff's new role at the firm and its seemingly endless obligations and late nights, with no end in sight, are beginning to take a toll on their relationship. When he became managing partner, Jen had told him, "Great! What you've done is won a pie-eating contest only to discover the grand prize was a lifetime supply of pie!"

So far, it seems she was right.

Jeff rolls silently into the driveway of his house, touches the HomeLink on his monitor, and glides into the garage. It is 2215. He walks into the house and puts his leather computer bag down in the hallway outside the door to his study. He's got more work to do but that can wait for a few minutes as he first checks in with his family.

He walks to the living room and sees Jen sitting with her legs tucked under her, a deep-blue throw over her lap. The 77-inch Sony OLED is on, the volume barely audible. Jen, who often has the TV on to keep her company, looks up from the book she's reading.

"Hi, babe."

"Hi, Jen. How was your day? How was Emma's game?" Jeff says, almost too quickly.

"My day was fine. The game was good. How was your day?"

Jeff senses an underlying current of . . . what is it . . . disappointment, disgust, frustration? He wonders if what he thinks he's sensing is actually there or if it's his guilt taking hold. Is it real or is he feeling it because he missed Emma's game, *again*?

"My day was stressful, busy, and disjointed," he says, as he walks to the bar to pour himself two fingers of Glenlivet 21. He glances over at Jen who isn't saying anything, but is looking at him intently over the rim of her readers. He realizes this act, coming into the house after a long day and heading to the bar to pour himself a stiff drink, has become almost automatic. And with the statistics on attorneys and drinking, he might want to revisit that habit. He smiles sheepishly at Jen and puts his empty glass down and places the bottle back in its place on the shelf.

"Where's Emma?"

"She's up in her room studying for tests she has later this week."

"I'm going to head up and say 'hi.' . . . Should I prepare myself to hear about missing her game?"

"What do you think?" Jen offers somewhat dismissively. She continues after a moment to allow her remark to sink in. "You know, actually, she didn't even mention it today on the ride home. She was awful quiet, though." She puts her book down on her lap. "Quieter than I've seen her in a while."

Jeff takes a deep breath, lets out a sigh, turns and heads upstairs to see his daughter. He pulls up short and gathers himself outside Emma's bedroom to steel himself against the anticipated storm about to consume him, and which, he believes, Emma has every right to thrust him into. He feels a larger-than-normal knot in his stomach as he knocks on the door. There's no response. He knocks a bit louder, and after still no response, he gently opens the door.

"Hey, Goosey," he says tentatively. He and Jen have called Emma "Goosey" since the day she was born.

The first thing he notices is her basketball uniform thrown in the corner. He sees Emma, her blonde hair still wet from the shower, sitting at her desk with her back to the door, wearing her new noise-canceling headphones. She doesn't respond and Jeff isn't sure if it's because she hasn't heard him or because she's upset about his broken promise to come to her game. Jeff's breath catches in his throat; in the light of her Apple iMac monitor and the lamp lighting her work area, Emma looks so much like Jen.

God he loves both of them. He loves them so much. *What the hell am I doing?* he thinks. *Why am I screwing this up?*

Daisy, the mutt they adopted from the Rancho Coastal Humane Society a few years ago, is lying on her bed next to Emma and lifts her head up, her tail thumping slowly. Emma looks over at her and lifts the left headphone from her ear.

"Hi, Dad," she says without turning around. Jeff hears an edge in her voice.

"Hey, Goosey. I'm sorry—"

She cuts him off. "It's fine," she says. "You're sorry you missed my game. Work was busy. You had an important project that needed to get done. Your day was crazy, there was so much going on. You really wanted to be there, but . . ." She begins to swivel in her chair to face him.

Jeff pulls up short. She completed his apology with such practiced ease, even getting his pauses and intonations spot on. He's even more disgusted with himself as he continues to walk forward and sits on Emma's bed. She turns fully around.

"I really *am* sorry, you know," Jeff says sincerely.

Emma doesn't respond. She is like stone; there's no reaction on her face at all.

"Tell me about the game," Jeff says.

"Oh, you know, it was fine."

Jeff feels like he's dealing with a hostile witness in court having to draw every syllable out of Emma.

"Who won?" he asks.

"We won."

"How many minutes did you play?" he says.

"I don't know, like twenty-five minutes."

"How'd you do?" he continues.

"Fine."

The knot in Jeff's stomach grows.

"Dad, listen, I've really gotta study. I've got some big practice tests this week in AP Calculus and History." Emma leans over, gives Daisy a scratch behind her ear. She begins to slowly turn around to face her desk and put her earphone back on.

"Hey, Goosey . . ."

Emma continues to turn back to her studies without saying another word. Jeff puts his hands on his thighs, stands slowly, walks over to her, puts his hands on her shoulders, kisses her on the top of her head behind the headband for the headphones and, more to himself than Emma, says, "I really am sorry."

He turns and walks to the door, glancing over his right shoulder. Emma's not looking at her desk; her head is down, her eyes focused on Daisy, her shoulders slouched. For the second time since he's walked into Emma's room, Jeff's breath catches. *Is she crying?* he wonders.

He closes Emma's door softly behind him, leans against the wall, and sighs.

This. This is all on him.

He turns and makes his way to his and Jen's bedroom, then to his walk-in closet. He glances up and sees the suits, starched shirts, and assortment of ties hanging neatly along the right side. As he gets changed out of his suit and into a pair of sweatpants and T-shirt, he catches a glimpse of himself in the mirror. He looks so damn . . . ? Empty? Tired? Sad? All of the above?

He walks downstairs, glances with disdain at his computer bag sitting in the hallway, and makes his way back to the living room.

"How'd *that* go?" Jen asks as she looks up from her book.

"Not great," Jeff says. He sits down on the couch next to her.

"I expect not," she says, placing a bookmark from Warwick's, the family's favorite independent La Jolla bookseller, into the book she's reading. Jen sets the book gently on top of the throw still covering her legs, folds her hands calmly on it, and looks up at Jeff as he continues.

"I was prepared for 'Hurricane Emma' when I walked in her room. I expected her to be angry, to lash out, to want her pound of flesh. Instead, what I got was so much worse. She was . . . resigned?" he says.

Jen remains quiet.

"You know, Jen, I really *am* sorry I missed Emma's game."

"I know you are," she says matter-of-factly.

"When she left work today, Pam asked me about Emma's game. I still can't believe I told her Emma would understand. What an ass I am."

Jen takes her readers off and puts them on the end table next to her. She still doesn't say a word.

"It's just . . ." Jeff trails off.

They sit quietly, each avoiding the other's gaze, for what seems to Jeff to be five minutes, but is probably no more than thirty seconds.

Jeff looks up and says, "The world believes I'm a success, but I'm not sure you, Emma, or even Daisy think I am. Shit, *I* don't know that I am. I'm certainly not reaching my full potential as a husband and a dad."

Jen begins to speak and stops herself. Clearly Jeff is not finished.

"Sure, I make a comfortable living, enough where Emma can go to The Bishop's School. We have this beautiful house. You and Goosey get to travel. But . . . there's something missing, Jen. I feel like the dream I had before I went to law school about what my life would be like as a lawyer is gone forever. I've lost the thread."

Jen listens quietly.

"And now, the collateral damage to you and Emma is almost too much to bear." Jeff stares out the window. "I wish there was something I could do to, I don't know, reclaim my life? Infuse more passion and purpose into my legal practice? Live with more joy and intention? All of those things?"

"Jeff, you've been a success at everything you've ever done," Jen says. "You're a brilliant man, a loving husband and dad. Yes, you fall short sometimes. Welcome to the human race." Her eyes lock onto his. "Since you became managing partner of the firm, though, you fall short here more than sometimes. And, you're right, Emma and I are collateral damage. The thing is, honey, I know you'll figure this out. But the clock on your relationship with Emma is ticking."

Jeff notices that although Jen doesn't say the clock on their relationship is ticking, the underlying subtext is clear.

"Isn't there someone you can talk with to help you figure out how to find what it is you're missing?" Jen asks.

"I can talk to my therapist," he says.

Jeff has been seeing a therapist for a few years now. "The thing about those discussions, though, is they make me feel better, but they don't necessarily help move the ball forward, you know?"

The conversation with Jen is almost too much for him to bear. He feels lost and worried he won't be able to find his way back. But he says none of that. Instead, he hugs his wife and thanks her for listening, grabs his computer bag, and heads to the study to get back to work. He closes the door softly behind him, walks over to the desk, and places the laptop in the middle. As he opens it with a sigh, he thinks, *Why in the world is my life like this? How did I get here?*

He stares at the computer screen and sighs.

"Fuck."

The day's refrain.

THE REST OF Jeff's week is the same—which is to say, it's filled with interruptions, the business of running the law firm and, when he could squeeze it in, legal work. Lately, each day feels like "wash, rinse, repeat." He wishes it weren't so, but he can't seem to change it.

On Saturday morning, Jeff and Jen are sitting at the kitchen table enjoying their fresh-brewed cups of coffee. On weekends, when they have more time, they switch from the Keurig and, instead, break out their Chorreador from Costa Rica. Jeff and Jen learned to make coffee using the device when they were in Costa Rica on a surf trip, more than a decade ago. It's been their Saturday morning ritual ever since.

"Hey, aren't you playing golf with the guys today?" Jen asks.

"I'm supposed to, but I've got this hearing Monday I've got to prepare for. I'm going to have to call Chuck, beg off, and close myself in the study for a few hours. It's a good thing we live in San Diego where another picture-perfect day is around the corner!" Jeff titters, but Jen's not laughing.

"Babe—" Jen begins.

He cuts her off more brusquely than he intends. "I know, I know. If I keep blowing the fellas off, they're going to stop even inviting me."

"I doubt Chuck would ever do that, you two have known each other for . . . going on ten years?"

"Gotta be."

"What I was going to say was, if you don't play a bit, what's the point of all of this?" Jen waves her extended left arm and hand in a circle around her head.

"I know, right? I've been thinking the same thing!" he laments. "What do you say we ditch this existence, head to Baja and lead simple lives of meditation, yoga, paddle boarding, surfing, and shrimp tacos?"

Jen looks at him over her readers. "You know they say there's a bit of truth in even the most hyperbolic statement, right?" She smirks. "If that's what you want to do, can we at least wait until Emma graduates from high school?"

"You know I love being a lawyer. I think I love it more than most. I'm not ready to hang it up quite yet. I'm still young despite my graying temples," he says seriously.

"I know you do," Jen responds. "Know we're a team. I support you no matter what. And, you know I love the shrimp tacos at that place in Todos Santos!" She giggles. "Do me a favor?" she asks seriously.

"Sure Jen, whatever you want," he says sincerely.

"Will you please go surfing tomorrow morning? I know how you love it; the feeling you get when you're out there on your longboard, communing with the ocean. You're a different person when you come back home from a surf, you know," she says with equal sincerity.

"You know, I was looking at the surf report, tomorrow looks good for a morning session," he says. "You got it. I promise I'll surf tomorrow. That'll serve as my motivation to get shit done today."

Jeff grabs his phone, gets up from the table, and calls Chuck to beg off from today's golf outing. Chuck is, of course, disappointed, but says he understands. Jeff walks back into the kitchen.

"Funny, Chuck didn't even try to change my mind." He can't help but think it's similar to Emma's reaction the previous night: resigned.

Jen is quiet and he wonders if she's thinking the same thing.

"Off on my thirty-second commute to the study. I'm going to close the door so hopefully I can focus and get my stuff done. Wish me luck!" he says with a joy he doesn't feel.

"Good luck, honey," she says with feigned enthusiasm.

He closes the door.

THE NEXT DAY, Jeff wakes without an alarm and is quickly up, out of bed, and ready to head to one of his favorite surf breaks, Tamarack, off Carlsbad. It's time to join the dawn patrol. *How long has it been since I've surfed a morning session?* he thinks to himself as he pulls into his parking spot. "Too damn long," he answers aloud.

Minutes later, he's in the water, fully present and engulfed by the elements. It's almost as if he's become one with the board and his board one with the waves. He feels exhilarated and free. Free of the oppressive, ever-present weight of the world on his shoulders.

As his session comes to an end, Jeff exclaims to the waves of the Pacific, the blue Santa Ana scrubbed morning sky, the birds, some dolphins who are riding the waves around him, and to the universe: "This feels so good! Why don't I do this more often?"

As he walks to his car, he realizes this was the first time in a long time he wasn't thinking of the pressures of being an attorney, serving clients at a high level alongside the duties he's taken on as the managing partner of his law firm. He also hadn't been despairing of how he's neglected his relationship with Jen and Emma or his friends. He felt a deep peace.

Jeff stops to pick bagels up for the family—a poppyseed with hummus for himself, an everything with lox and cream cheese for Jen, and an onion with cream cheese for Emma. He makes his way home. He walks in the house, where he can hear Jen and Emma speaking in the kitchen. As he walks in, the conversation abruptly stops.

"Were you talking about me?" he says with a hint of fear.

"As a matter of fact, we were." Jen looks at him.

"Okay, spill the beans. I'm strong. I can take it," he says with a bravery he doesn't feel at all.

He slides into a seat at the breakfast bar and hands out the bagels. They each unwrap their bagel in silence. An uncomfortable tension hangs over them like fog over the beach.

Jeff sighs. "Honestly, what gives? Give it to me straight," he says.

"Dad . . ." Emma stops and begins to tear up.

Jen looks at Emma, then at Jeff. "Emma and I were talking about the other day," she says.

"It's okay, Goosey, talk to me," he says with deep emotion.

"It's just that . . ." Emma stops herself again, looks down at her bagel and takes a bite, unable to get the words out.

"She's really upset, right, Emma?" Jen offers.

"Yes. You know, it wouldn't have been so bad if you hadn't promised me you'd be there," Emma says, still looking down at her bagel.

Jeff puts his bagel down on his plate. He's still feeling the endorphins from his surfing session and isn't upset about where this conversation is going. In fact, it ought to have happened long ago. He's also glad Jen is letting Emma find her voice.

"I know. Believe me, Emma, I know," he says.

"So, please don't promise me you'll be there, and I won't get upset if you're not," Emma offers.

The words hit Jeff like a Mike Tyson left hook to the gut. He's speechless which, for Jeff, is as rare as San Diego snow. He wants to be there for Emma, always. And he tells her he'll be there for her, always. His actions, on the other hand, say something different.

"Emma, honey. I completely understand. I really do. As your grandma used to tell me: 'Jefferson, there are *reasons* and there are *excuses*; it is critical for you to know the difference,'" he says. Now it's his turn to look down. "I think I've learned the difference and can tell you that anything I say about the other day would be an excuse."

The three of them sit in silence for several beats. The only sound is Daisy's tail thumping the floor next to Jen.

"You know, your mom told me the other day that she believed in me and I'd figure this out. Do you believe that?" Jeff asks, hungry for her to express her belief in him.

"I don't know," Emma says honestly.

Another Tyson punch to the gut. "Will you give me a chance?" he asks.

"Okay," Emma says unenthusiastically.

There's a pause and Jen adds quietly, "Okay."

"Okay," Jeff says.

He's tied in knots. They don't believe him but are throwing him a bone at least.

He doesn't know how he'll figure it out, but looking at Emma and Jen, he decides to dedicate himself to finding out.

Chapter 2

A Chance Encounter

"The definition of insanity is doing the same thing
over and over again and expecting a different result."

~ ATTRIBUTED TO ALBERT EINSTEIN

It's Tuesday morning. As he drives up the 5 toward Los Angeles, with 91X playing on the radio, Jeff thinks to himself, *At least Emma doesn't have any basketball games today for me to miss!* He grimaces.

The conversations with Jen and Emma last week are still weighing on him. He's never had conversations like that before with Emma.

He thinks back and what bothers him the most is her seeming resignation about the situation. It's like she's given up on him. He thinks about his conversation on game night with Jen. *I haven't opened up to her like that in what feels like forever. It felt good. Why don't I do that more often?* he muses.

His mind pivots to work. Jeff is required to report his continuing legal education (CLE) credits this year and, as usual, despite Pam's reminders, he's left getting his credits until close to the last possible minute. Now today's the day to take care of it.

He's heading up to Irvine for meetings this afternoon, will take some clients out to dinner tonight and then attend an in-person

CLE tomorrow. He may even squeeze in a visit to his brother's place in Huntington Beach. It's been a while since he's seen him and the kids.

He probably could have done the meetings and CLE remotely, but after his conversations with Emma and Jen, he thought some time away to think would do him some good. Plus, he's hopeful the energized feeling he gets connecting with colleagues at CLEs will somehow help him find his way.

The day's client meetings go well—they were glad to see him and thankful for the opportunity to sit at a table with him after all the usual Zoom meetings or telephone conferences. In-person meetings do make a difference, in Jeff's estimation. He also had a nice dinner with a client before fitting in more work at his hotel. Unfortunately, he didn't make it to his brother's house. *I need to make that a priority.*

The next day, Jeff walks into the ballroom for the CLE seminar. It's been a good trip away, but by now he can't help thinking about how much work is piling up while he's gone. He really doesn't have time to be out of the office all day, and is already considering taking the hit on his CLE total and leaving at the lunch break to get back. On top of all of this, there's still the nagging pit in his stomach when he thinks about Emma. *Something has to change*, he thinks to himself.

Jeff tries to focus on the morning sessions, which are interesting, but it's hard to settle in. His phone keeps ringing, and he can't stop himself from constantly attending to his inbox. He can't keep his attention on the speakers.

And his distraction is noticeable. At least it is to Amy Thorngood.

Amy is a co-managing partner of the Los Angeles office of Smith Bartholomew, Jones, and Knight, an Am Law 100 firm. By chance, she sat behind Jeff and a few seats to his left. Because they're on the left side of the ballroom, he's in her field of vision as she watches the presentations. And, unlike Jeff, she *is* paying attention.

As she watches him glued to his phone, she grimaces and thinks, *I used to be the way that guy is. I don't know how I survived! Oh, that's right . . . of course I do . . . barely!*

About five minutes before the next scheduled break, Jeff gets up to again answer a call. He puts his phone to his ear, says "Hold on a minute," and excuses himself as he slides past the four other people sitting in his row between him and the exit.

Amy watches him walk out of the room, then turns her attention back to the speaker who's finishing her presentation on leveraging technology to become more efficient. When the master of ceremonies for the CLE takes the stage to announce a fifteen-minute break, Amy gets up and makes her way to the water cooler by the door. She refills her water bottle and walks out into the hallway. She sees Jeff sitting on a bench staring off into space.

Jeff certainly isn't the only attorney at the conference who is distracted and on their device. But something about him is tugging at Amy. *Why am I compelled to introduce myself to this struggling stranger? What's the deal?* she wonders. Could it be because, as she paints a picture of this stranger's life in her head, she sees something in him—true or not—that reminds herself of another attorney she once knew? Herself.

She's guessing he's around the age she was when she first became a co-managing partner. It's a fair bet given not only the volume of distractions he's had during the presentations, but also the graying of his hair. She also sees his wedding band. *I bet he has kids too,* she thinks. She mutters to herself, "Why am I imaging him being in the exact spot I was when I first became co-managing partner?"

That period of Amy's life was challenging to say the least. And maybe life is nothing like that for this man. But she's drawn to him because her imagination has clicked in, and right or wrong, she has a sense he too might be at a crossroads. Like she was. Amy feels he might be at a potentially life altering decision point, where maintaining the status quo could result in catastrophe at work and at home . . . maybe the same crossroad Amy was at when she, with the help of a coach, took her life back? These thoughts run, no speed, through Amy's head in a matter of milliseconds. She makes a decision. She'll introduce herself, as much out of a sense of service as curiosity. Have her powers of observation and intuition painted an accurate picture, and this is an attorney who she can serve? Maybe show him his work doesn't have to be all-consuming, frantic, and soul-sucking? Or is she telling herself a story that's totally off base?

Amy begins to walk toward him to introduce herself, but is waylaid when another attorney stops her progress for a chat. She and Jeremy have known each other for years, and although she is happy to see him, Amy is a bit disappointed when she looks over Jeremy's shoulder toward Jeff and sees he's on another call.

The CLE organizers send representatives out into the hallway to announce the end of the break. Amy turns to enter the ballroom; this next presentation is one of the main reasons she chose this CLE and she doesn't want to miss it. She glances over her shoulder at Jeff and vows to meet him at the lunch event in a few hours.

As Jeff returns to his seat, he sighs. He spent the entire break putting out fires. The calls were incessant and the emails filled with other people's priorities.

Jeff's priorities for the day had been to connect with his colleagues, learn things to help him in his practice, and maybe, just maybe, get some relief from all of the things he must do as the managing partner of GH&B. Instead, his day is worse than it would have been had he stayed back in his office in San Diego. He decides he'll definitely cut out and head back to San Diego at the lunch break. At least in the car he won't be able to check his email.

The second CLE block of the morning is no different for Jeff. He's again constantly checking his email and has to leave the ballroom three times to take calls. When the MC announces the lunch break, Jeff stands up, determined to head to the parking deck, get in his car, and head back to the office. He's got work to do and laments the fact he chose to come to this CLE. He could have stayed in his office and done online education or, better yet, could have registered for an on-demand event and watched it on 2x speed on a Saturday—and gotten more out of it than he's gotten out of this.

As he walks toward the ballroom door with his laptop bag and blazer under his arm, Amy approaches him.

She extends her hand. "Hi! I'm Amy."

Jeff stops. "Oh, hello. Jeff."

"How's the CLE treating you?" she asks.

Jeff looks down at the ground. "Honestly, I've been working so much I haven't gotten much out if it!"

"I hear you! It can be tough to get away from the office and really focus on learning." She grins. "Can I buy you lunch?"

Jeff looks up at her more closely and chuckles. "Isn't lunch included in the CLE?"

"Ah, you caught me! I'd love to have lunch with you next door and find out more about you. I'd like to hear your story."

"Really? I was about to leave and head back to San Diego . . ."

"Oh, you're up here from San Diego? I have a daughter who lives in Encinitas! I spend quite a bit of time down there," she says cheerfully. "Come on, you already paid for lunch, let's at least sit together and get to know each other a bit better. Isn't that the best part of in-person events like this? Meeting colleagues, building our networks, and getting recharged for the battles we face as lawyers?" She grins.

Jeff hesitates for a moment, thinking he really should leave and get back to San Diego. But when he looks up to see Amy patiently waiting, he gives in to his gut, which is telling him he should stay.

"Okay, you've talked me into it. I'd enjoy getting to know you, Amy. Besides, I'm suddenly starving. I'd have to stop at In-N-Out to get an Animal burger, fries, and a chocolate shake for the road, and probably make a mess as I drove south!" They both crack up.

Amy and Jeff walk through the buffet line, find a table with some space, and take their seats.

"So, Jeff, what's your story?" she asks.

"What do you mean? What I do for work, my personal life? What? That's such a broad question!"

"That's up to you! I purposefully ask it that way to let you pick."

For some reason, Amy makes Jeff feel comfortable and at ease, as if they've known each other for years. Jeff takes a bite of his sandwich and sighs.

"Honestly, Amy? I'm at my breaking point. I know, as lawyers, we're not supposed to admit that, but it's the truth. I'm a new managing partner at GH&B in San Diego. That role, along with the legal work, has me juggling so many things, I never seem to be 100 percent dedicated to anything. It also has me missing some of the most important times in my daughter Emma's life. She's seventeen, by the way." He looks away from Amy. "By all outward appearances, I'm successful, whatever that means. But I don't feel that way. I know I'm not reaching my full potential as a leader, lawyer, husband, father, community member. If there's not a better way of doing all of this life, I—I'm not sure I want to continue to be a lawyer . . ." Jeff's voice trails off, then he looks back at Amy. "Crap, I'm sorry, I barely know you!" Jeff wonders why he said all that to a total stranger, especially when lawyers aren't supposed to show weakness among their colleagues.

Jeff looks down at his plate and takes another bite of his sandwich.

Amy looks at Jeff with empathy and understanding. "There's nothing to be sorry about, Jeff. You had something to say and you said it." She goes quiet until he looks at her. "Don't think for a minute I asked the question as a throwaway! I wanted to hear your story, that's why I asked. I don't have time to ask questions and only pretend to want to know the answer."

Jeff looks at her and thinks, *Who the hell is this woman?*

"Look, believe it or not, I get it! I'm the co-managing partner at Smith Bartholomew here in Los Angeles."

"Oh! Of course I know SBJK. You guys are *big*. How many people are in your Los Angeles office?"

"I think we've got around 300 lawyers in our office here. Worldwide, we've got more than two thousand."

"Holy cow! I had no idea." Jeff shakes his head.

"Yep. When you and I get to our level, it's a whole new ball game, right? There's so much more to being a managing partner than we imagine. The leadership responsibilities, and the business of the law, making sure the lights stay on and people thrive. Add to that the actual 'lawyering' and it can be a lot!"

"That's for sure! I've got a difficult enough time at GH&B, I cannot imagine what it's like managing an office the size of SB! How do you have time to even be here? I mean, really here. I don't think you've checked your phone once since we began talking. Mine has been buzzing in my pocket almost nonstop.

It's all I can do to not excuse myself and deal with it." He shakes his head again dejectedly.

"Oh, I know your phone's been buzzing. I'm really glad you haven't excused yourself though." She grins. "It wasn't always this way for me. When I first realized I was on the track to become a co-managing partner, I had no idea all it entailed. When I spoke with Rob, my husband, about it, he told me becoming a co-managing partner was like winning a pie-eating contest only to discover the grand prize was a lifetime supply of pie!"

"Are you kidding me? My wife said the exact same thing," Jeff says.

They both laugh.

"I was overworked, stressed almost to the breaking point, headed toward burnout," Amy says. "I, like you, was getting to the point of pitching it all. I'd find something else to do that wasn't as stressful. I even thought of opening a fish taco stand in Baja!"

Jeff laughs. "Me too!"

"But I love being a lawyer! I truly do. I think the law is a noble profession. You know, not too long ago—looking at you I'd guess it's within both of our lifetimes—mothers and fathers were proud to tell people their daughter or son was a lawyer. Somehow, some way, our profession has gone from that to being a punch line. When people who don't know us ask what we do for a living, there's a hesitancy, even if for a beat, before we tell them . . . if we even tell them."

"I know! Crazy, right?" Jeff is suddenly *very* interested in what Amy has to say and is glad he listened to his gut. "So how'd you figure it out?"

Amy starts to laugh. "I'm not sure I've 'figured it out,' Jeff. I'm trying to be better every day, but 'figured out'? I don't know about that." She's thoughtful for a moment.

"I'm sorry, I interrupted you. Please. Continue." Jeff waves his hand.

"Anyway, one night I came home late, again. I've got two kids. They were fourteen and sixteen at the time. When I walked in the house, Rob and the kids were hanging out in the living room watching something or another, a football game, perhaps. I stopped at the doorway and stared at them. They hadn't heard me come in from the garage. I thought to myself, 'What the hell is it all for if I can't be a real part of this family?' You know?" she says seriously.

"Oh, believe me, I feel you," he says.

"The next day, Rob and I were out walking our yellow Labrador and I began to open up to him. Rob is a C-suite executive at a mid-market manufacturing company, Excelsior. Have you heard of it?"

"I haven't," Jeff says.

"Anyway, we were out walking and I was ruminating—you know, verbally processing. Rob looked at me and said, 'Why do you think you *have* to do this alone?' I, of course, told him I wasn't. I had a team of people helping me. He wasn't buying it."

"Anyway, Rob continued and told me that even though I had an undergrad business degree, I'd learned the business of law and leadership through the school of hard knocks. And that school of hard knocks I'd attended? Filled with shitty instructors, people who had to try and learn the same way I did." Amy stopped to let Jeff absorb what she was saying.

Jeff thinks about Zoe, the former managing partner at GH&B. Was she a lousy instructor?

Amy continues. "Rob told me what laggards lawyers could be. Being in the corporate world, he knows lawyers are slow to pick up on new tools and opportunities. He asked me again why I thought I had to do it alone. I told him I wasn't, that I had a co-managing partner to help with the load. 'That's not what I mean,' he said. He told me about how in the corporate world, which is light-years ahead of us lawyers stuck in the Stone Age, they had borrowed a page from outstanding athletes and started using coaches to empower their evolution, get out of their own way basically, and reach their full potential. He reminded me that he had worked with a coach for years. And I did know that, of course. But I'm a lawyer for Christ's sake. I thought I could figure it out on my own or get by with a little help from others in the field."

Jeff nodded. "Right." Of course he knew about coaching. He'd been the assistant coach of Emma's YMCA basketball team ten or fifteen years ago. He'd even heard Bill Gates talk about the power of coaching. But he'd never heard of a coach for people like him, specifically for lawyers.

"So I told Rob that lawyers are *different.*" Amy snorts. "And he asked me, 'How so?'" When I couldn't answer, he started reeling off a list of names who felt the need to have a coach. Sundar Pichai, you know, the CEO of Google. Sheryl Sandberg. Jeff Bezos. They have all teamed with a coach. Bill Gates, Bill fucking Gates, who has a TED talk about the *need* to have a coach. He asked me why in the world I would think lawyers are different."

"I read about Bill Gates and his thoughts on coaching," Jeff says. "I've never heard of a coach for people like us though, Amy."

"That's the thing, isn't it? A coach for lawyers? Who'd heard such a thing?" She smirks.

"Anyway, I came up with all sorts of reasons for Rob which, of course, were nothing more than excuses. No one will want to coach me. I'm not coachable. I'm already busy enough, how in the world do you expect me to take valuable time out of my day for something as woo-woo as coaching? No one will understand what it's like to be a lawyer, and if they do, they'll be a terrible coach. I don't have the money for coaching. You name it, I had an excuse for it."

"So you didn't hire a coach? What did you do to find the secret?" Jeff asks sincerely.

"Oh, no, I hired a coach. In fact, I still see him today. We've been working together for around seven years off and on." She counts the years on her fingers.

"Wait. You're telling me there are coaches out there who work with people like us?" Jeff says with a bit of shock in his voice.

"It turns out there are many coaches out there, Jeff. Some of them even work with people like us!" Amy grins and turns serious. "A select few will not only work with people like us, but they'll understand how challenging things are for us because of our legal training. You know, our brains don't work the same way as other people."

"I know! My wife is constantly telling me to 'stop being such a lawyer'! If I had a dollar . . ." Jeff trails off.

"Right?" Amy says. "Well, here's the thing. I'm not sure if our brains were like this and that's why we went to law school, or law school made our brains this way . . . you know, a kind of chicken and egg situation . . . but however it happened, our brains are programmed to be hyperanalytical, hypercritical, hypervigilant, and to see risk, almost all risk, as bad."

"Yes, of course you're right. We see monsters under the bed, and when we grab a flashlight and look there, there aren't any. We don't accept that and instead believe they must've simply moved to the closet."

They both laugh.

Amy continues. "Finding the right coach for people like us is even more critical than for others, I'd say. Perhaps that's my ego talking, but I don't think so." She eats a forkful of salad.

"Yes, I found the right coach for me and hired him. It's been life-changing really."

"I'd ask you for his name and contact information, but . . ."

"Oh, I know! That's a bridge too far, amirite?" She chortles.

"Yes, you are most definitely right . . . I've got so many thoughts running around my head about this I can't begin to tell you."

"That's the excitement of believing there can be a way for things to be different. For you to reach your full potential," Amy observes. "Here's the thing though, working with a coach, especially a coach like mine, is a no-nonsense proposition. The work is challenging. I'd freely call some of our sessions intense. You have to be in the right place to work with any coach, but especially one who works with managing partners like you and me." She sips her sparkling water. "I'll tell you another thing. On top of all the excuses I had for Rob about why coaching could never work for me, I had one more. I was frightened." Thinking back on that feeling, Amy can't help but snicker and shake her head.

"Me," she says, "the co-managing partner of a 300-attorney office for a global powerhouse of a law firm. Me, a person who had reached the pinnacle of her career. Me, a lawyer who had a stellar reputation among the bench and bar. Me, a person who was making, let's face it, ridiculously good money. I WAS SCARED." Her voice is serious.

"What were you scared of?" Jeff asks.

Before Amy can answer, they hear a voice come on the intercom, announcing the afternoon session in five minutes.

"Shit!" Jeff exclaims. "I was so enjoying our conversation. This is the reason I came here in person today. Well, not this conversation exactly, but to connect with colleagues and recharge my batteries."

"I know! I really want to catch this afternoon session, though.

One of my best friends is presenting and I promised him I'd be there." Amy begins to rise.

"Oh. No worries. Of course! I've taken up enough of your time as it is. Thank you for telling me there's a way." Jeff stands up and starts gathering his things.

They start to walk toward the door; Amy stops. "Jeff, I grew up in Missouri, you know, the 'Show Me' state. I am a complete and total evangelical for the power of coaching and what it can do for folks like us. Lawyers with almost incalculable potential, but without the ability to unlock it on our own."

Jeff looks on quizzically, uncertain where this is going. "Please don't give me your coach's number. I'll feel terrible when I don't call him," he says seriously.

"I wouldn't dream of it. I'm not sure you're the right fit for him anyway."

"So how will you 'show me'? You've got about ninety seconds before you have to head back in," Jeff says.

"I'll be down in San Diego next Monday. As I said, my daughter lives in Encinitas. I'll be visiting her over the weekend. I'll stay over until Monday and you and I can meet to continue our conversation. What do you say?" she asks with a lightness he doesn't quite comprehend.

"I couldn't ask you to do that!" he says.

"You haven't asked me to do anything. I volunteered."

"Um. Well. I don't know," Jeff says hesitantly.

"What is it?" Amy asks. "You don't know if you'll have the time? Or is it something else?"

"It's the time, yeah. It's also, well . . ." Jeff goes quiet. If he's being honest with himself, he's afraid, like Amy had been.

They start walking again.

"Meet me next Monday at Better Buzz on the 101 in Encinitas. Do you know where that is?" Amy asks.

"Of course I do. I live up the freeway a bit in Carlsbad."

"Okay. Meet me there at 7:30 a.m. on Monday. You can buy me a coffee and we can continue." She offers her hand.

It seems to be settled. "Okay, Amy. Better Buzz on the 101 in Encinitas next Monday at 0730 hours," Jeff repeats. "I'll see you there, I guess."

"Yes, you most definitely will," Amy replies. "Now, I've gotta scoot and get in there. My friend will know if I'm not. See you Monday!"

With that, Amy turns and walks into the ballroom. Jeff turns the other way and walks out of the hotel. It's time to head back to San Diego and the mountain of work that has surely piled up on his desk in his absence. As he pulls onto the on-ramp, he thinks to himself, *What just happened?*

As he drives, Jeff tunes his satellite radio to a classical music station and allows his mind to wander. He cannot stop thinking of how Amy seemed to have it all together and he doesn't. "Is that a consequence of her being further along her path than me?" Jeff mutters out loud.

He's on internal autopilot as he drives down the freeway, past San Juan Capistrano and Dana Point and San Clemente and the twin domes of the decommissioned San Onofre nuclear reactors. Jeff wonders whether he can actually get "there," to the place Amy appears to be, or if it is a pipe dream and he's destined to suffer the fate of so many lawyers. To have a life of "good enough" as a managing partner, and perhaps a husband, father, and person in general. He knows he'll never settle for that state as a lawyer.

Why am I willing to settle in some areas of my life and not others? What does it say about me that I would never settle to be a mediocre attorney, and yet, truth be told, I'm doing that in virtually every other area of my life? He's not entirely comfortable with the question.

He continues down the freeway past Camp Pendleton and Oceanside, past his exit and on down the 5. His thoughts speed through his mind like the traffic on the 5; he can't, nor does he want to, stop them. Thoughts about how he wants to live his life, how, if he's being honest, he's half-assing things that most definitely shouldn't be half-assed outside of the office. As he drives past Mission Bay Park and Old Town San Diego, his wonder begins to turn to frustration. *Damn it, I'm a smart guy. Why can't I figure this out? I've been able to figure stuff out all my life.*

As he pulls into his space in the parking deck for his office, Jeff makes a decision. Whatever it takes, he's going to change.

The thought invigorates and frightens him.

I sure hope Amy is at Better Buzz on Monday. I need to find out her secret.

Of course, the office isn't on the same page as Jeff. It doesn't really care about what he wants, at least not yet, and it's certainly not going to allow him any grace to try and figure things out. Not this minute.

He walks in and is instantly waylaid by Jonathan, who says impatiently, "I emailed you, why didn't you get back to me?"

"Whoa!" Jeff exclaims. "I was at a seminar and on the road to get back here." He disciplines himself to take an audible breath and consciously tells himself to remain calm and relax his body. Finally, he reminds himself to remain curious.

"Must be nice to be able to get out of the office . . ." Jonathan mutters.

Jeff ignores this and walks with Jonathan into the Trestles conference room. He looks at the photograph on the wall of the surf break near San Onofre. He had just driven by it and didn't even notice because he was so in his own head wrapped up in thought. He sighs as he takes a chair. "What can I do for you Jonathan?"

Jonathan remains standing. "I've gotten wind another associate may be leaving us. Why does this continue to happen?" Jonathan says with exasperation. "F'ing millennials," he says. "We need quality associates who stay at GH&B for the long term."

Jeff, gobsmacked, looks at Jonathan with bewilderment in his eyes and more than a few thoughts, which go unsaid, in his head. "That's what was so urgent?"

"Yes. You need to do something about this. You're the managing partner!"

Jeff looks at Jonathan, the firm's head of human resources, who's job responsibilities include, among other things, finding and recruiting top talent for the firm as well as employee satisfaction and retention, and thinks to himself, *I need to do something about it?!* To Jonathan, he simply says, "I'll look into it."

Jonathan turns abruptly and leaves the conference room. As he leaves, Jeff hears him muttering, "Whatever . . ."

Jeff takes a deep breath and stares at the photo on the wall, wishing he had gone surfing instead of coming back to the office.

In the past, Jeff might have become short with Jonathan, which would have resulted in more wasted time and hard feelings. He was glad he kept his cool today.

A few minutes later, he stands up and walks out of the Trestles conference room. When he gets to his office, Pam looks up from the work she's doing. "What in the world are you doing here? I've got you out until tomorrow morning. You were scheduled to be at that seminar all day. Plus, it's 4:30!"

"I know, Pam," he says sheepishly. "Honestly, I wasn't really getting much out of the seminar with all the calls I was taking and the emails I was responding to."

Pam looks at him with a raised eyebrow. "Calls? Who was calling you? I know I didn't, and I didn't put anyone through to you."

Jeff looks embarrassed. "Well. That. For the past few months I've been giving a few select clients my cell so they could get hold of me in an emergency."

"Jefferson!" she admonishes. "Why in the world would you do that?"

Jeff knows he's hit a nerve. She never calls him by his full name; at least she hasn't in a while. "It seemed like a great way to engender a feeling we were different here at GH&B. You know, to differentiate us from the others," he says. "Pam, there are so many attorneys, both good and bad, out there. I thought if a client wants to contact me, I should be available to them 24/7."

Pam looks at him as they enter his office. "There are many ways GH&B separates itself from the competition. We're great at what we do. We have a team atmosphere. We provide tremendous value to our clients. Why in the world would you think giving your clients your cell number would be a good idea?" she says unbelievingly. "That's taking a very important person out of the chain: me!"

"I know . . ."

"Is that why you didn't tell me?" she asks.

Jeff looks at her and feels like he's seven years old and is explaining himself to the principal of his elementary school. "I didn't tell you . . . because I knew you'd tell me not to?"

"Your darn right I would have! Look. We've worked together for how many years now?"

"Must be fifteen?"

"Closer to twenty, I think. Anyway, if you're afraid to tell me something like that, what do you think Jen would say about such a harebrained idea?"

Jeff looks down at the tops of his well-shined shoes and mumbles, "I haven't told her either."

"Of course you haven't! Now that clients have your number, you can't take that back." Her tone softens, but not by much. "*Please* don't do that anymore, okay? Other people's emergencies aren't necessarily *your* emergencies. I'm good at figuring that out, so let me do my job."

"You're right. I'm sorry. In my mind, it had nothing to do with you and everything to do with client satisfaction," he says. "I blew it."

"Well, think about it this way. If you have your clients believe you're at their beck and call 24/7, you can only miss one call and you've failed because that's what they'll remember," Pam states.

"I hadn't thought of it that way."

"I didn't think you had! But enough of that. It's done. How can I make the remainder of your day as productive as it can be?" she asks.

"Can you please get me the Mulegé file? I want to start getting prepared for that arbitration," Jeff says as he sits down behind his desk.

"Of course!"

When Pam comes back in with the file, Jeff asks, "Hey, have you ever heard of Amy Thorngood? She's the co-managing partner up at Smith Bartholomew's LA office?"

"Of course I have. Her admin Waylon and I are friends from way back. Why do you ask?"

"I ate lunch with Amy today before heading back. Our conversation got me thinking about a lot of things," he offers.

"According to Waylon, Amy is the best. She's got her stuff together. Now, that is." Pam looks at Jeff seriously and lowers her voice conspiratorially. "From what I know, though, it wasn't always that way."

"Well, as you say, she appears to have it together now," Jeff says. "Okay, thanks. I'm meeting her for coffee Monday up in Encinitas to try to learn her secret."

"From what I hear, you couldn't have a better person to speak with," Pam says.

Jeff turns in his chair, looks out at the Coronado Bay Bridge, and wonders if Amy gives clients her cell number. He thinks to himself, *I'll have to remember to ask her Monday.*

Chapter 3

It's All on You

*"The best years of your life are the ones in which
you decide your problems are your own . . . You
realize that you control your own destiny."*

~ Albert Ellis

It's Monday morning, 7:30 a.m.

After a weekend visit with her daughter and several great surf sessions at various locations along the San Diego coast, including a quick one this morning at Swami's, Amy is sitting at Better Buzz on the 101 in downtown Encinitas.

The sun is shining and the large garage-door windows are fully opened. Amy sits in the front corner at a small table for two. She loves the spot for the 270-degree view it affords her; while sitting on the bench seat, she can see out the windows to her left and across the entire coffeeshop. She checks her watch and wonders if Jeff will show. He was harried last week, but seemed to want to learn more about how she had, to use his words, "figured it out."

As she watches the early-morning work crowd grab their coffees for the drive, she thinks back to how her life was so much like Jeff's when she first became a managing partner. Trying to juggle all the balls, regardless of whether they were Waterford crystal or a Super Pinky rubber ball, and regardless of whether the thing was at work or at home. Trying to do everything, which she now knows is not humanly possible, and burning so bright, burnout was a forgone conclusion. *What a difference having an objective set of eyes and ears has meant to me*, she thinks. She looks at her watch and realizes she should have given Jeff her cell phone number.

JEFF IS INCHING down the freeway, and panicking. He thought he left his house in plenty of time to make it to Better Buzz by 0730 hours, 0740 at the latest. Things are not, however, going according to plan.

First, he couldn't find the key fob for his car. Then he remembered Monday is trash day and had to move the cans to the curb. Of course, one of them always gives them trouble because it has a bad wheel. Ultimately, he was successful in muscling the can down the driveway to the curb, but it sucked a few more minutes of his time.

When he got on the ramp to get on the 5 South, it was backed up. That was his first clue the commute wouldn't be smooth. Because he was distracted by looking for his fob and getting the trash cans to the curb, he failed to check the traffic report. Had he done so, he would have seen there was a crash on the 5 between Leucadia Boulevard and Encinitas Boulevard. A truck hauling onions south overturned and was blocking the travel lanes. Traffic was being directed onto the shoulder, resulting in a huge backup.

As Jeff crawls down the freeway, he thinks to call Amy, remembering he doesn't have her number.

He finally gets to the Leucadia Boulevard exit and it's now two minutes before seven. He takes the exit and heads west toward the 101. *This should only take ten minutes. I'm still good*, he thinks. Then he crests the hill and looks down.

Unfortunately for him, the traffic on the 101 is much worse than normal too. Apparently, others had the same idea he did. His hands tense on the wheel and he feels himself begin to grind his teeth. After the traffic light cycles for what feels like the one hundredth time, he finally is able to turn left on the 101 to begin his crawl south.

By the time he gets to Better Buzz and finds a place to park two blocks away, it's 0745. *I hope she's still there*, he thinks as he begins to run back north to their meeting place.

AMY GLANCES AT her watch again. "7:50. Well, I guess he's not . . ." She looks up. The door opens and Jeff hurries through.

"I am so sorry I'm late! I would have called, but I didn't have your number!" he says.

"As I was sitting here I was kicking myself for not giving it to you last week." Amy stands up to greet him with a smile and a warm handshake. "I was beginning to think you were going to blow me off! I was about to get my coffee to go and hit the road back to LA."

"I'd never blow you off. The traffic on the 5 was a mess, an accident, I guess. Some onion truck overturned. I got off at Leucadia to come down the 101 and it was even worse! I guess everyone had the same idea. I'm really sorry!"

Jeff rushes through his explanation so quickly Amy doesn't even bother to try to understand most of it. She does wonder, however, if Jeff took a breath between what she imagined were sentences. She takes a breath herself. "What you experienced this morning brings up a good point of discussion for today, if you're game."

Jeff looks at her a bit confused. "I thought you were going to tell me how you figured it all out?" Jeff wants tactics, checklists, tangible things. He doesn't understand, not quite yet, what Amy has in mind.

"Jeff," she guffaws, "remember, I'm from Missouri. I'm more about showing than telling. But first, let's get our coffees. I'm also going to get one of those good-looking banana-nut muffins. I'm hungry after my dawn patrol session at Swami's today. It was short, but definitely sweet."

"Wait, you're a surfer?" he says, with a hint of surprise in his voice. He didn't picture someone in Amy's position to have any time for what he, at the current moment, considers frivolity.

"Yep, sure am. I've been surfing for about thirty years. Why are you surprised? You know darn well people of my 'vintage' surf, right?" She smirks as she says this.

"Of course!" Jeff exclaims, embarrassed. "That's not what I meant at all! I meant surfing is something that takes time out of anyone's schedule, and you're, well, you! You've got a law firm to run." He pauses for a moment, thinking to himself how he views surfing as a luxury he doesn't have the time for today and really hasn't since he became managing partner. "I'm a surfer as well. I'd like to get out on the water more, but . . ." Jeff trails off.

"But the work, always the work," Amy finishes, laughing. "You know, I was kidding with the 'vintage' comment. Second, the busier I am, the more things I have on my plate and the heavier those things seem, the *more* surfing helps me." She looks at him closely. "Jeff, it's when we believe we can least afford time to do an activity, whether it be surfing, meditation, going for a walk, a date night with your wife, the more we should lean into doing exactly that. You're no good to anyone, least of all your clients, if you don't."

Amy and Jeff walk to the counter to place their orders. She orders a coffee and that banana-nut muffin, while he orders an Americano and a chocolate muffin. They walk back to the table by the window. As they make small talk, Jeff is thinking of Amy's statement about leaning into the personal stuff he doesn't think he has time for. What strikes him the most is, well, when he thinks about it, she's right about needing those things to be at his best for his clients.

As they sit, Jeff says, "I'm really sorry for being late this morning. I've been thinking about our conversation the other day and looking forward to this meeting. I really want to learn how you figured it all out."

Amy replies, "Oh, I'm definitely a WIP, you know, a work in progress. The key I learned from my coach is to move forward a bit each day on creating the life I want to have and to, ultimately, reach my full potential as a human being."

"Wait, if you haven't figured it out, what hope do I have??!!" he says. Although he tries to muster a bit of humor as he says this, it doesn't come across. He really believed Amy would be able to give him a checklist, he could go through it, and his life would be better. Maybe he put too much hope in this meeting.

"Don't compare your beginning to my middle, my friend," Amy says calmly. "We all need to learn to crawl, then walk, then run. That's also a lesson Jessie drilled into me."

"Who's Jessie? Your coach?" he asks, as the barista announces their orders.

"Yes, he's my coach. I'll get our stuff, you sit here and get ready to explore something that may blow your mind," she says as she gets up and retrieves the coffees and muffins with a nod and a "thank you."

Amy walks back to the table with the orders and takes her seat. "Blow my mind?" Jeff says as Amy places the coffees and muffins on the table. "Really?"

"Well, we'll see," she says as she takes a sip of her coffee. "Before we get started though, tell me about a win."

"A win? What do you mean? At work, at home? That's a pretty open-ended question, Amy." Jeff is being difficult and he knows it; Amy knows it. He feels out of his depth. He's also thinking he should have declined the offer to meet. He wonders if he should fake a call, excuse himself and say he's got to go to the office, and call it a day. He's not sure why, but he is once again feeling a bit frightened.

She nods. "It's open-ended and broad for a reason. That's how I roll, remember?" She snickers. "Now, turn your lawyer brain off, stop analyzing, and pick something you consider a win."

"A win . . . well, I guess a small win would be the fact that after I left the seminar last week, I didn't lose my cool when Jonathan, the firm's chief human resources officer, confronted me. When I got to the office, he was in my face about staffing, recruitment, and the fact he had gotten wind an associate was going to be leaving GH&B. There were two things that seemed really crazy to me: first, he was pissed I hadn't immediately responded to the email he sent me as I was driving and, second, he seemed to want me to do his job for him. So, I am proud of remaining calm in the tempest that was Hurricane Jonathan."

"First of all," Amy begins, "there are no small or big wins, like there are no small or big losses. They are wins. Don't qualify or quantify them. The qualifiers are the story we tell ourselves around what it is we did. The fact is, you didn't lose your cool with Jonathan. Period. You consider that a win. Period."

"Okaaaayyyyy," Jeff says as he takes a bite of his chocolate muffin. This conversation isn't going anything like he had pictured.

"Seriously, try to get out of that habit. Believe me, it's a tough habit to break but it's worth it." Amy is dialed in and can see that Jeff, despite his Herculean attempt to remain calm on the outside, is struggling. She's not surprised. She experienced what she presumes are feelings similar to what Jeff is experiencing when she first began working with Jessie. She sips her coffee and allows a bit of silence to make its way into their conversation.

The silence doesn't last long. Jeff is not only frightened, he's stressed, and so, he's impatient. "Is that what will 'blow my mind'?" Jeff uses air quotes here.

"No." Amy pauses and breaks off a piece of her muffin. Before she pops it into her mouth, she says, "Tell me about something you learned about yourself through that experience."

"What did I learn about myself? I don't know . . ." he says off-handedly. At the same time, he thinks to himself, *Seriously, what is this? What's going on here?*

Amy again allows some space for Jeff and lets the silence hang. She allows the question to sit and for Jeff to think.

"I can remain calm with Jonathan the same way I remain calm with difficult clients," he finally admits.

"Are you asking me or are you telling me?" Amy sips her coffee.

"Ha ha. Very funny. I'm telling you," Jeff says with mock indignation.

"Awesome! Congratulations on your win and the thing you learned about yourself. It's by stacking up wins day-in, day-out, and continuously learning about ourselves that we move forward."

"Something Jessie taught you?" Jeff asks.

"Jessie, and my mom, Barbara," Amy replies.

Jeff takes a bite of his muffin. "Let's get to the thing that may blow my mind, please! I'm dying here!" Jeff exclaims.

"Have you ever heard of the concept of extreme ownership?" Amy asks.

"I think I may have, but I'm not sure," Jeff replies hesitantly. *Is extreme ownership the key to me figuring it all out?* he thinks to himself. He's grasping for something tangible to hold onto in this conversation.

"Let me ask you this," Amy begins. "Why were you late to our meeting this morning?"

"Oh, that's easy," Jeff exclaims. "The traffic was heavier than I expected because of that damn onion truck. Everyone had the same idea. I had to get off the freeway and come down the 101. Parking was impossible, so I had to find a spot a few blocks away."

Amy looks on, bemused. "Anything else?"

Jeff takes a deep breath. "Also, the traffic lights here on the 101 all have this odd timing thing that throws everything off when there's a Coaster train coming through Encinitas."

"Anything else?"

"Nope, I think that's it . . . Oh, wait, there is one other thing; make that a few other things. I couldn't find my fob, that took a few minutes. It's trash day and I forgot to take the cans out last night. Plus, one of the cans has a busted wheel, which we know about, but we haven't gotten around to contacting EDCO, the waste management company. So, that delayed me."

"Any other reason you were late this morning?" Amy asks.

"No, I really think that's it."

"Jeff, I'm sorry to say all of that is, well, bullshit." Amy looks at Jeff expectantly. She knows what's coming before Jeff opens his mouth. She also knows it's probably been a while since anyone has called Jeff out like she did.

"No! It's all true! I swear! Those are all the things that happened this morning! I got up in plenty of time to make it here by

0730, 0740 at the latest." In his head, he adds, And *who the hell is this woman anyway to tell me all the things that made me late to our meeting are bullshit?*

"You didn't finish that thought," Amy says.

"Huh?" Jeff responds, bewildered.

"Well, you didn't add 'in a perfect world.' In a perfect world, I would have made it here for our 7:30 a.m. meeting, no later than 7:40."

Jeff looks at Amy, but says nothing. He thinks, *Is she right? Was I operating as though everything should go perfectly smooth and I'd get here on time? How reasonable is that?*

"You know, Jeff, when I was growing up, my mom used to say: 'Amy Kari, there are reasons and excuses.' What you gave me Jeff were a bunch of excuses."

"Wait a second! First of all . . ." Jeff begins indignantly, but trails off.

Amy raises her left eyebrow ever so slightly.

Jeff gathers himself and starts again. "My mother used to say the same exact thing. Just the other day, I shared that sentiment with my daughter, Emma, when I was speaking with her about missing one of her basketball games. But Amy, all the things that happened this morning were totally out of my control. I don't think I am making excuses."

"Oh, but you are," Amy says plainly. "Let me ask you this: What if you had planned on being early for our meeting today? After all, I couldn't help but notice you left yourself no margin for error. You said it yourself; you were planning on getting here, what did you say, by 0730, 0740 at the latest?"

"I'm just so dang busy! I was up late last night in my home office working on stuff . . . are those more excuses?"

"Let's get back to my original question. Have you ever heard of the concept of extreme ownership? It means there is absolutely no one, or no thing, to hold responsible for the results you achieve, what some people call consequences, but yourself. You're late for our meeting? That's on you." She looks at him seriously. "Extreme ownership means you own everything in your world. Every single consequence you experience, whether positive or negative, is a direct result of decisions you've made."

Jeff looks on with unease. "Okay. I should have planned on being here at, like 0725. I get it. But the traffic and stuff, there's no way I could have accounted for that. I wasn't responsible for any of it." He's still fighting; he can't see where Amy is going with this and he's uncomfortable because, as an attorney, he likes to be two or three steps ahead of the competition. And that's how he's viewing Amy in this moment—as the competition.

"Hang with me here, Jeff. Turn off your lawyer brain," Amy says with a knowing grin. "I know it's hard, we're trained to assess risk as an external thing. Our decision-making is almost entirely risk based." Amy continues, "I never said you were responsible for any of the events this morning. But now that you mention it, let's take a look."

"Sounds great," Jeff says, with what will soon be revealed to be misplaced confidence.

"We'll start with what you said to me last. You were up late last night. That was a decision you made, correct?"

"Well, you see . . ." As Jeff begins to tell a story about why he absolutely had to stay up late the prior night, Amy, who's not having any of it, holds up her hand. She recognizes she's dealing with a trained professional who has a narrative deeply engrained in his mind, which is currently incapable of understanding extreme ownership. The two of them actually make great sparring partners.

"Jeff, I'm not trying to be mean here. This concept is fundamental to moving forward, so it is critical we at least crack the door open to it," she says. "Let me ask it this way. Yes or no, did you decide to stay up late last night, or did someone, for example, take you or your family hostage, hold a gun to your head, and force you to stay up late, presumably working?"

Jeff snickers. "Well, of course we weren't taken hostage like in one of those Liam Neeson movies!"

"Right, so it was a decision. You would agree with that premise, wouldn't you?" She looks straight at him.

Jeff is fighting as hard as he can to think of a way he can disagree with the simple statement but cannot. "Yes, it was a decision."

"What led to that decision is a road we needn't go down at this point. Stay with me here," she says.

"But why not?" he laments. "Isn't the reason I had to make the decision the least bit important to you?"

"Honestly," she says, deadpan, "no." She takes a bite of her muffin followed by a sip of her coffee, all the while allowing the silence to settle between them. Jeff is, again, seriously questioning what he was thinking meeting with Amy.

Amy finally speaks. "Would you like to know why it's not important?"

"That would be great," Jeff says with more than a hint of scorn.

Amy ignores the scorn; she knows Jeff is feeling confused, and likely a bit overwhelmed, at the moment. "I don't want to hear the story because, well, we *all* have stories behind why we chose to do one thing or another. There's usually a story behind the story, and so on and so on, ad infinitum." She lets what she said sink in. "Also, for the purposes of this discussion, what led to you feeling like you had to decide to stay up late is irrelevant."

"We all have a story," he says quietly. "I suppose that's true."

"Good. Now keep your lawyer brain off for the next little bit, please."

"I'll try, but it's not easy!" he says, a bit less guardedly. *Maybe this conversation is going somewhere useful after all*, he thinks.

"I know, trust me! I've got a lawyer brain too, remember! . . . "So, what was one result of that decision?"

"Well, I suppose that, because I was working, I forgot to do my chores and take the trash to the curb."

"Excellent. What else?"

"I was tired this morning and couldn't find my car fob. Wait, that's not right. I couldn't find my fob because I didn't put it where it normally goes. That's the place for it at night."

"Go on," Amy urges him. "What are some other results of deciding to stay up late?"

"Because I was up late, I didn't get up early enough for there to be a buffer to get here early."

"Anything else?"

"Not that I can think of," Jeff says hesitantly.

"Are you certain?" Amy asks.

"Well, I suppose because I woke up late, and didn't leave enough time for a buffer, I didn't check the traffic report. Had I done so, I would have known about that damn onion truck."

"And . . ." Amy has her full-on direct examination hat on, coaxing information out of Jeff so he'll have the opportunity to make the connections for himself.

"And . . . I could have found an alternate route to our meeting here and made it on time."

"And . . ."

"Honestly, Amy!" Jeff says smiling. "I feel kind of like I'm on the witness stand!"

"Sorry. That's the litigator in me!" They both share a hoot, and the tension Jeff was feeling eases, but only just.

"Okay," Amy says. "Connect the dots. Are you beginning to understand what the concept of extreme ownership means?"

Jeff pauses before he answers, not certain of himself. "I think so," he finally says. "I've got to own the consequences of each and every decision I make."

He pauses to sip his coffee, considering what he just said. "When you get right down to this morning, what that means is it all started with my thought of getting here at 0730. Everything really flowed from there."

He turns his head to look out the windows into the clearing San Diego morning, pondering whether this thing, this concept of extreme ownership, helped Amy on her own path.

"That's right. The consequences you suffer, or for that matter reap, are all on you. Period. As a leader for your law firm, and as the pilot for your life, extreme ownership is a concept that will get you far in creating the law firm, law practice, and life outside of work you want to have. It sounds harsh, but it actually gives you back your life." She pauses and sips her coffee, noticing Jeff appears to be deep in thought and struggling with something.

Jeff looks down at his half-eaten muffin. "I get the concept, but it seems so dependent on the willingness and ability to spend the time evaluating each decision and all of its potential consequences. Isn't that a time-sucking rabbit hole?" he asks. *And,* he thinks to himself, *I don't control everyone else in the world.*

"That's one way to look at it, Jeff," she offers. "Another is to come to understand time invested in this way will pay dividends because you'll be aware of the second- and third-level consequences of the choices you make. It will take you from reacting to situations to responding."

"What does that mean?" Jeff wonders aloud.

"Do you remember taking your daughter Emma to the pediatrician when she was young?"

"Of course. Because I was so busy, I wasn't able to make every appointment, but there were times that I did." Jeff has a thousand-yard stare as he looks out the window remembering.

Amy holds some space for him before asking, "What are you thinking about?"

"Oh, just the fact that I missed so much of Emma's stuff because of my work," Jeff responds quietly. *Too damn much.*

"I know. I get it. I was the same," Amy continues. "There's a Chinese proverb that goes something like this: 'The best time to plant a tree is twenty years ago, the second best time is today.' Don't beat yourself up too much. You can't change the past, but you're here today, planting your tree now."

"I guess you're right," Jeff says and snaps back to reality. He looks at Amy. "What were you going to say about Emma's doctor visits as a kid?"

"Right. Well, do you remember when the doctor would test Emma's reflexes by hitting her knee or elbow with a reflex hammer?"

"Of course! Somewhere in the deep recesses of my mind, I recall a doctor doing that to me as well."

"Well," Amy continues, "when the knee was struck in the spot the doctor hit it, did Emma or you have any control over whether your leg jutted out?"

"Nope. It didn't matter how hard I tried to stop it either."

"Exactly." Amy nods. "That's a reaction. There's no thought to it. It just happens. When choices present themselves and you make decisions, the same thing is possible. You can react without thought of the potential consequences, like a doctor hitting your knee with that hammer, or you can respond by thinking of the consequences, the immediate ones which often relieve the pain in the short term, and the secondary and tertiary ones which may result in more pain in the future. Reacting versus responding."

"I'm beginning to get it, I think," Jeff muses.

"Let me ask you this, Jeff," she says. "Do you see yourself as being in 100 percent control of your life?"

"100 percent control? Of course not. That's absurd. Is anyone in 100 percent control of their lives?"

"Tell me more," Amy says with a curiosity that surprises Jeff.

"You really are curious about this, aren't you?" Jeff asks. "Well, it's not really possible for me to be totally in control of my life. I've got a wife and daughter. I have a law firm to run, and you know what all that involves on a much greater scale than I do. I've got clients and their needs. Not to mention the courts and their requirements on my calendar. Let me ask you the same question, Amy. Do you see yourself being in 100 percent control of your life?"

"As a matter of fact, I do," Amy says with a grin.

"How in the world is that possible?" Jeff wonders. "You've got a husband, two kids, and you co-manage a law firm. How can you actually be in full control of your life?" he asks.

"Jeff, it's all about mindset, which creates our self-perception. That's it. If you believe you are a person who is in 100 percent control of your life, guess what? You'll become a person who has much more control over his life than you ever thought possible." She sips her coffee in silence watching Jeff struggle with this concept.

"It cannot be that simple," Jeff opines as he shakes his head and stares straight at Amy.

"Oh, but it is. Simple, however, does not mean it is easy," Amy says. "What we've really been talking about is your attitude around a concept known as locus of control. At its base, this is a question about whether you believe things happen *to* you and are the result of things that are outside of your control or whether things that happen are a consequence of the choices you've made.

Psychologists call the first an 'external locus of control,' the second, an 'internal locus of control.'"

"I think I'm beginning to understand," Jeff says hesitantly. "What you're saying is it's important to change the way I think about things and switch to having a disposition for an internal locus of control." Jeff sits up a bit straighter, thinking, *Now we're getting somewhere, even if it does sound kind of woo-woo.*

"Yes, and it is important to recognize it will not happen overnight," she says. "We lawyers are results-driven animals. This type of work, though, takes an investment of time and effort. As I said, it is simple, but it is not easy." Amy feels Jeff's engagement has picked up. She can tell she's hit on something a bit more tangible for Jeff to consider.

"You must've been reading my mind!" Jeff exclaims. "I was just thinking of how I could flip the switch today and change my life," he says.

"Trust me, when Jessie and I had a discussion around extreme ownership and locus of control, that thought came to my mind." Amy chuckles. "Want to know the other thing that I thought?"

"Absolutely," Jeff responds.

"I thought talk of mindset was . . . a bit out there for me."

Jeff doesn't respond. He does, however, wonder if his face had betrayed his thoughts.

Amy continues. "Jessie warned me about mindset work being simple but not easy, but I wouldn't listen. You may find out I'm a bit hardheaded when it comes to some things. Anyway, my failure to believe Jessie led to some tough moments where, at some points, I was ready to chuck the entire shift and go back to the way I was." She sighs. "I mean, I was successful by the world's standards before I hired Jessie, I'd be successful by those same standards if I failed at shifting my philosophy."

Now it's Amy's turn to have a thousand-yard stare as she is

transported back to her early work with Jessie. She lifts her coffee cup to her lips, takes a sip, and shakes her head as she puts it down on the table.

"That's the beauty of having a coach though," she continues. "Jessie reminded me of the fact that success isn't the world's to define, it was my job to define it for myself. And I had hired him to coach me because I didn't view myself as being as successful in the ways I most wanted to be." She grins. "The whole thought of chucking it was nothing but me wanting to throw in the towel because this thing, which I felt should be so easy, was so darn hard. So I lied and told myself it wasn't for me."

Amy snaps back to the present and finishes her coffee. "I learned that perspective is a muscle you must build over time. It is most definitely not like a light switch. You get to go to the "gym" every damn day and work on the muscle. Over time it becomes stronger and stronger. Eventually, it will run in the background most times, but occasionally you'll have to stop yourself and bring it to the surface when you're making a decision under stress, because that is when the pull of your old reactionary habits will be the strongest. When your brain perceives stress, you're in fight-or-flight mode and totally catabolic. You don't respond, you react."

Jeff nods in agreement. "I can totally see that happening; the part about my reactionary habits coming back to rear their ugly head." He takes one last bite of his muffin and a sip of coffee. "Damn, that muffin was delicious!"

"I know, right?" She smirks. "Listen, reacting in the moment isn't always bad. Think about swerving on a highway to avoid a catastrophic collision. Don't get me wrong, there are times when you've got to react. The fact of the matter is, though, living a reactionary life most of the time results in a lack of control and a lack of growth."

"I can see that," Jeff agrees, as he finishes off his coffee.

Jeff notices Amy glance at her watch for the first time the entire morning. "I've kept you long enough. You've left me with a lot to think about," he says.

"If you have a few more minutes, I'd like to share one additional concept and then we can wrap up until next time," Amy says.

"Next time?" Jeff says.

"Oh, yes, next time, if you believe it will be valuable for you." Amy had noticed Jeff easing into the dynamic of a coaching relationship; he was tense at times, likely pushed back internally a whole bunch, but now, as their meeting comes to a close, she sees someone different sitting across the table. Someone more open. And something about sharing what she's learned has felt really good too.

"Valuable?" Jeff exclaims. "Of course! I've gotten so much out of our time together this morning and I can't thank you enough. I don't want to impose on your time, though. I know you're busy." Jeff looks on sheepishly.

"Listen Jeff, I told you my daughter lives right up the street. I'm here often. I'm enjoying our time together, sharing what I've learned from my work with Jessie. I'm not a professional coach. I view my role here as potentially getting you to a place where working with one would bring you the most bang for your buck," Amy says.

"That sounds great. How can I repay you for something like that?" Jeff asks.

"We'll get to that sometime. Don't worry about it!" Amy replies. "For now, let's get to the final concept for today. So far, we've talked about extreme ownership and internal locus of control. Another way to talk about mindset is within the framework of what the professionals call a 'fixed' versus a 'growth' mindset."

More with mindset? Jeff wonders.

Amy snickers. "You're thinking more woo-woo stuff, right? But I can tell you, a growth mindset approach combined with extreme ownership and adopting an internal locus of control will make all the difference in how you approach leadership as a managing partner, how you approach your law practice, and how you approach your life."

"Really?" Jeff says. "Okay. Tell me more."

"This stuff comes from Carol Dweck's work," Amy begins.

"I haven't heard of her," Jeff responds.

"She's a psychologist up at Stanford who's known for her work on motivation and, you guessed it, mindset," Amy says. "We're tight on time, so if you're interested in diving into the details of what I'm about to share, pick up her book *Mindset*."[4]

"Okay, got it. So what's her biggest takeaway?"

"The main thing on this I've learned through reading Dweck's book and my work with Jessie is that a person with a fixed mindset has some 'go to' phrases that hold them back. For example, they'll tell themselves 'my potential has a predetermined ceiling,' or 'when I fail, I am at the limit of my abilities and can't ever push past that point.' A person with a fixed mindset also doesn't receive feedback well and often views it as criticism."

"That doesn't sound great," Jeff responds. "It seems like having a fixed mindset can lead to an unhappy and limited life." He pauses. "Admittedly, sometimes I'm not great at receiving feedback. I take it too personally."

"We all do, my friend," she says. "On the other hand, a person with a growth mindset believes they can learn to do whatever they want, and view failure as a temporary condition and an opportunity for growth. They look at feedback as information to use to grow and improve, not as criticism." Amy looks at Jeff. "That's enough for today."

---

4 Carol S. Dweck, *Mindset: The New Psychology of Success* (Ballantine Books, 2007).

"I feel like I've been drinking from a fire hose this morning, Amy," Jeff says. "I don't know how I'll tackle all of these concepts and improve. I don't even know where to start!"

"Let me ask you this," Amy says. "What's your greatest insight from our time together today?"

"Let me think for a minute," Jeff says as he stares out the window. "It's got to be the concept of extreme ownership. Every decision I make has three levels of consequences: immediate and anticipated, secondary, and tertiary, which may not be anticipated or even considered."

"Okay," Amy says. "Given that insight"—she continues looking intently at Jeff—"what are you going to do about it? Because knowledge without action is such a freaking waste."

"I'm going to try to be more aware of the long-term consequences of the choices I make," Jeff says.

"Not good enough," Amy challenges. "That's too squishy. Make it concrete!"

"Okay," Jeff says. "How about this? I will pick one decision per day I am going to make and write down that decision and the potential immediate, secondary, and tertiary consequences before acting."

"Right," Amy says. "I'm looking forward to hearing how you've done. I'll be back down here four weeks from now. Want to do 'same bat time, same bat channel?'"

Jeff looks on quizzically. "If you mean, here at Better Buzz four weeks from today at 0730," he says pulling up his calendar, "that works for me!"

"Different generation," Amy mutters. "Great, I'll see you then . . . and don't keep me waiting next time," she says, still smiling.

"Oh, I won't. It's all on me, right? . . . To be safe, what's your cell so I can text you if I'm running behind?"

Amy gives him her number. "One more action step for you, Jeff, if you're game."

"Of course I am," Jeff exclaims.

"Text me your email today and I'll send you an assessment to measure your disposition around locus of control," Amy says. "It's simple and won't be a heavy lift for you at all. Don't overthink it, be honest. Email it back to me when you've completed it and we'll talk about it next time."

"Sounds great. Thanks!"

They walk out of Better Buzz into the warming Encinitas morning. As they say goodbye, Jeff says, "Hey, Amy, thank you. Although I feel a bit overwhelmed, I haven't felt this optimistic about things in a long time."

"¡Con mucho gusto!" she exclaims. "It is my great pleasure."

She turns left and heads toward her car, then calls over her shoulder, "See you in a month, and don't forget your homework! I'll be asking about it first thing."

As Jeff heads toward his car, he wonders why Amy seems to care so much about him and his success. He can't be sure, but he knows he's thankful.

WHEN JEFF ARRIVES at GH&B, Pam is waiting for him. One of Jeff's most needy clients had "stopped by" to speak with him without an appointment or any notice. While Pam apologizes, Jeff pauses a moment to consider how this situation had come to be. The concepts of extreme ownership and internal locus of control are starkly present in this moment.

"Pam, it's not your fault. This is on me. I've created a relationship where Sally believes showing up here without an appointment is acceptable. I'll own this," he says as he pats Pam on the shoulder, sighs heavily, and heads to the conference room where Sally is waiting. As he walks down the hallway, he resigns himself to the apparently guardrail-less situation he's created with Sally.

A few hours later, his email client chimes, notifying Jeff of the arrival of a new message. He stops what he is doing and opens his email to see a message from Amy. It's the "Locus of Control" assessment. He shakes his head and laments the fact he was distracted by the email notification, and forces himself to get back to work. He'll leave the assessment for another day. First, though, he takes out his phone and begins his list of identified opportunities to exert extreme ownership over the decision to leave the assessment for now and any resulting potential consequences. He arrives at: he's good with it.

Later in the week, Jeff has a scheduled meeting with GH&B's leadership team to begin planning for the next quarter. He's in the conference room ten minutes early, having purposefully blocked an additional fifteen minutes at the front end of the meeting so he wouldn't work right up to the meeting's start time. When the appointed time for the meeting to begin arrives, Jeff urges everyone present to grab their seats so they can begin.

Andrew, the head of the firm's tax group, interrupts. "Aren't we going to wait until Robert arrives?"

Jeff considers the question. "We'll give it a couple of minutes. We're all busy and I certainly appreciate each one of you arriving here in time for the meeting to begin on time. It's only when we begin on time that we can possibly end on time. When we start late, it creates a cascade of events that has the ability to throw us all off schedule."

Robert enters the conference room out of breath. Jeff has a flashback to his entrance at Better Buzz earlier in the week for his meeting with Amy. He's interested in whether Robert will take extreme ownership of why he's a bit tardy for the meeting.

"Welcome to the meeting, Robert," Jeff pokes, with a grin. Before he has the opportunity to say anything else, Robert interjects. "Sorry I'm late everyone! I was tied up on a call with a client who wouldn't let me hang up the phone!" He looks around the table as if to enlist all of the participants to his way of thinking. "You know how it is."

Without missing a beat, Jeff adds, "Of course we know that feeling. We're going to get to the agenda because, as I said before you arrived, if we don't begin on time, we won't end on time. If we don't end on time, each and every one of our days will be thrown off track. I know all your calendars are as booked as mine." He pauses for a moment. "At my next standing meeting with each of you"—here he makes eye contact with each of the leadership team present as only an elite trial lawyer with years of courtroom experience making eye contact with jurors can— "we'll discuss a concept I learned this week, which I think could have a monumental positive effect on the firm."

The others look at Jeff and then at each other. Jasmine speaks up and asks what most, if not all, the others are thinking. "What? What is it and why can't we get into it now? It sounds important!"

Jeff grins and nods his head. "It is important. However, it's not as urgent as the items on our agenda today." He dims the lights, touches a control, and the agenda appears on the 80-inch high-definition monitor on the wall. "Let's stay focused, address the things we came to the meeting to address, and move on with our days. I promise I will create time in each of our schedules to talk about the concept. Trust me." The others turn their attention to the agenda and get down to work.

Over the coming weeks, Jeff does, indeed, introduce the concept of extreme ownership and internal locus of control with his leadership team at GH&B. Their reactions are varied but Jeff appreciates the openness most of them bring. He knows if the leadership team universally adopts the philosophy Amy taught him, the culture of the firm will be much improved.

Jeff isn't, however, only thinking of extreme ownership and internal locus of control at the office; in the days after his meeting with Amy, he tries to keep them front and center (or at least in his mind) outside of the office as well.

One weeknight he phones Jen to see if she and Emma might be free to meet him for dinner in La Jolla. Jen checks the family's electronic calendar. "I'm sorry, hon, we can't meet you tonight. Emma's got a thing."

Although Jeff would have loved to have met his girls for dinner, and is disappointed, he's not upset. "Hey, Jen, there's no need for you to be sorry! I know how busy you and Emma are, and I shouldn't leave these kinds of requests to the last minute. It's totally on me."

Jen is quiet for a moment. "Honestly, I know how upset you usually get when you suggest a spur-of-the-moment thing and we can't make it . . ."

"I know, I know," Jeff says, feeling a bit ashamed. "Do you remember what I shared about extreme ownership and internal locus of control, the stuff Amy told me about a few weeks ago?"

"Of course I do," Jen says cheerfully. "I think adopting that type of ethos might be a game changer for you and GH&B."

"Me too," Jeff quickly responds. "The thing is, I think adopting that frame of mind will help me in situations like dinner tonight too."

"How so?" Jen asks, unsure where the conversation is headed.

"I know how busy you and Emma are," Jeff begins. "It's not reasonable for me to put the onus on you to be available every time I have a wild hair. It's entirely on me. If I ask at the last minute, I've got to own the outcome, which, in this case, is a no."

Jen is both relieved and moved. She and Jeff have been together for a while. The fact he used the exact phrase she was thinking in order to frame his response is continued proof of their connection. "Jeff, that's a helpful way of thinking about this type of thing."

"I know," he responds, with deep caring in his voice. "When I think about it in these terms," he continues, "it becomes clear the only person to be upset with is, well, me, for not asking sooner. But I can't really be upset with myself because I didn't know I'd have the urge to meet you and Emma in La Jolla for dinner tonight."

"When you get home tonight, let's get something on the calendar for all of us. We can find a day to meet you," Jen offers.

"Sounds like a plan, babe. I'll see you tonight. I promise I won't be too late."

They hang up the phone. Jeff pauses for a minute and gives himself a silent kudos for taking ownership of the situation.

The Saturday before his meeting with Amy, Jeff suddenly remembers he hasn't completed his "Locus of Control" assessment. "Gawd dang it!" he exclaims, drops his head and takes a deep breath. He was hoping to not go into his home office at all today and, instead, spend quality time with Jen, Emma, and Daisy. "Nah, nah, dude," he says out loud to himself. "Own this. You didn't make it a priority; you made decisions which resulted in where you are now." Surprisingly, after saying this, Jeff feels better. Is it because he's more empowered by his newly evolving and strengthening mental framework and his understanding that, indeed, each decision he makes (or neglects to make) has a myriad of consequences, some obvious, others not so much.

As he sits at his desk and opens the computer to complete the assessment, two thoughts run through his mind. First, *How many times over these past four weeks have I* not *seen the opportunity to exercise this mindset muscle?* And, *Will I ever be able to have the mentality all the time?*

He gets down to business and takes the assessment. He's not sure what it all means or whether he has aced it; the lack of knowing makes him somewhat uncomfortable as he opens his email client, drafts a quick note to Amy, and attaches the assessment file. "Well," he says out loud as he is about to hit the "send" button, "here goes nothing!" With a whoosh, the email is off into the ether on its way to Amy. Jeff stands and heads out to the garden to help Jen.

Chapter 4

Beliefs Built on Lies

*"In crowds it is stupidity and not mother
wit that is accumulated."*

~ Gustave Le Bon

Two days later, Jeff drives down the freeway on his way to meet Amy. As he drives, he is thinking of the assessment and the concepts of extreme ownership and internal locus of control. Reflecting on the past month, he, of course, focuses on the times he failed to think about the secondary and tertiary consequences of decisions he'd made. *It's totally natural for me to focus on where I've fallen short,* he reminds himself, *but I've had some wins as well.*

Jeff flashes back to an incident when Sophie (the head of trusts and estates) buttonholed him with a question about a potential lateral hire. According to Sophie, the attorney under consideration was talented and had a wealth of knowledge and experience in trusts and estates. When she checked around with her contacts in the community, however, Sophie did not receive the best feedback regarding the attorney's interpersonal communication skills. She'd heard "great lawyer, but has trouble keeping assistants." When Sophie asked her assistant, Faye, about any interactions she'd had with the potential new hire, Faye was less than glowing.

"I've interacted with him on a few different occasions, Sophie, and, honestly, he was a bit abrasive."

As Jeff exits the freeway, he considers how he walked Sophie through the immediate consequence of having a skilled lawyer on the team, and the possible secondary and tertiary consequences of the effect on the trusts and estates team and GH&B as a whole having someone lacking interpersonal communication skills. The decision whether to hire the lawyer or not had not yet been made, but Jeff is proud how he took the time to guide someone else through the process. He just wishes he was better at doing it himself. *Isn't that always the way? I'm so much better when I'm guiding others than I am on following my own advice. But look, it's a process! Rome wasn't built in a day.*

He gets out of his car, looks at his watch, and begins to sprint toward Better Buzz.

It's 7:30.

At that precise moment, Jeff sprints past the windows and runs in the door. He checks his watch. "Damn, four minutes and thirty-seven seconds late," he exclaims as he approaches Amy. "I'm sorry, again!"

"No worries, Jeff. What was it this morning?" Amy asks with no trace of emotion on her face.

Jeff takes a deep breath. "It was totally me. There was traffic, but not a crazy amount; nothing like an overturned onion truck or anything," he says with a grin. "But I'm not blaming the traffic. It's as simple as I hit the snooze one time; that snooze lasted nine minutes. Had I not done that, I would have been early!" he says. Unlike his breathless excuse a month ago, he's now calm, measured, and confident.

Amy beams. "Now that's what I call extreme ownership! Let's get our coffees." She stands and joins Jeff for the short walk to the counter. The same barista from last time stands at the counter ready to take their orders. "What can I get you two?"

"I'll have an Americano," Amy says.

"Make mine the same," Jeff chimes in.

After they order food as well, the barista begins to turn to the next customer in line. Jeff asks, "Don't you need our names for the order?"

She says, "Oh, I know you're Jeff and she's Amy. I'm good with names."

Jeff is astonished by people like the barista; he is not good with names.

"Besides," the barista continues, "Amy is a regular here, so I really only needed to remember your name, Jeff."

Amy turns to the barista. "Thanks, Molly."

Amy and Jeff make their way to their table. "Tell me about a win," Amy says, as she slides onto the padded high-backed bench.

"How'd I know you were going to ask me that?" Jeff snickers as he settles in. "Oh, that's right, you told me you would." He pauses to think for a moment. "I'd have to say my win is leaning into the concepts of extreme ownership and internal locus of control, and completing the assessment you sent me."

"Tell me more, that's kind of squishy. What does 'lean into' mean to you in this case?" Amy asks.

"Boy, you don't let anything slide, do you?" Jeff grins.

"I listen and am curious!" Amy says proudly. "And what's measured can be improved, Jeff. 'Leaning into' something isn't measurable," Amy says.

"True enough!" Jeff says. "How about this, you remember my action step, right?" Jeff asks.

"Well...I remember you had several action steps...I remember all of them." She sits back. "Are we talking about picking one decision per day, writing that decision down, and considering the immediate, secondary, and tertiary consequences?"

"To consider those consequences *before* acting," Jeff adds. "Well, I was able to do that and it made a difference," he says.

"That's great!" Amy exclaims.

"Don't get too excited, Amy," Jeff says. "When I checked last night, I only did it ten times. It's been twenty-eight days since we last met. That means I'm batting less than five hundred," Jeff says.

"Nope, nope, nope," Amy chides. "Don't do that! Remember, no 'small' wins, just wins. Period. You did it, that's what matters! Besides, if you were a baseball player and that was your batting average, you'd be in the Hall of Fame," she exclaims.

Yeah, but . . ." Jeff trails off. "How can I win when I missed the mark more than 50 percent of the time?"

"Listen, did you expect to be perfect right out of the gate?" Amy asks.

Of course! The task wasn't all that difficult, and I'm a lawyer for heaven's sake. I do hard things all day long. But he keeps his thoughts to himself and smiles sheepishly. "Well . . ."

"I get it! You and I are quite a bit alike. I'm just further along on my journey than you."

Molly's voice rings out: "Jeff and Amy, your orders are ready."

"I'll get them," Jeff says, and gets up from the table. He walks toward the counter, reminding himself of the thought he had when he got out of his car this morning. Rome wasn't built in a day. He wonders why he's so freaking hard on himself.

"Thanks, Molly," Jeff says as he grabs the coffees and food.

He puts the coffees and food on the table. "Hey, Amy, can I ask you a question?"

"Of course," she says with a grin.

"Is it normal for me to feel like a failure at this point?" He looks at her seriously. "Logically, I understand what you're saying about just getting started and all, but, if I'm being honest, I'm not pleased with my results on the action step."

Amy takes a deep breath before beginning. "Honestly, Jeff, it *is* absolutely normal . . . Listen, we lawyers abhor losing. You feel like you lost."

"I do," he interjects.

"Let's remember the growth mindset stuff we talked about at the end of last time. Do you remember?"

He considers the question for a moment and a grin begins to appear. "Every failure is temporary and an opportunity for growth?" He doesn't sound sure of himself.

"That's correct," Amy says assuredly. "In fact, if we have a growth mindset, we stop categorizing things where we fall short as failures." She pauses to let her statement sink in. "You're not pleased with your results; fine. That does *not* mean you failed, it simply means you didn't execute properly. Think how to improve your performance on the list to continue to build the muscle." She grins. "You don't have to do that in the moment. Invest some time on it when we're not together, and think about what you've learned and how to leverage that learning to improve your performance."

"Hmmm," he says as he takes a bite of his muffin. "I'll do that." As he finishes chewing, he asks another question. "Why are you doing this? Why are you taking the time to help me? We aren't friends, although I can see that changing over time. So, why me? What gives?" Jeff asks.

"Before we get to that," Amy says, "tell me what you learned about yourself since we last met."

"What did I learn about myself . . ." Jeff looks out the window and takes a sip of his still-scalding hot coffee. "Well, I suppose one thing I learned about myself is I'm not much different than my kindergarten self."

"Tell me more," Amy says with open hands and an inquisitive expression.

"When I was tracking my action step, I got a jolt of excitement and satisfaction when I was able to put a check mark to signify I did it. When I remembered too late, I was upset and thought about taking my ball and going home."

"Why do you think you felt that, what did you call it, jolt of excitement when you gave yourself a check mark?" Amy asks.

"Frankly, I'm not certain," he admits. "I've never thought about it."

"We're all like that, Jeff," Amy says. "We love to check the box, get the gold star, stuff like that. When we approach that moment of checking the box, the anticipation of that, our brain gets a hit of dopamine."

"Wait, what?" Jeff asks. "Dopamine?" He was about to take a sip of his coffee, but places the cup back on the table.

"Yes, that's right. That good feeling we get when we know we're going to check off small goals results in a release of dopamine in our brain."

"Really?" Jeff asks, a bit surprised. He lifts his cup and blows on the still-steaming contents.

"Yep. That hit of dopamine helps us achieve our goals," Amy replies as she takes a bite of her muffin. "Congratulations on your win and your learning about yourself, Jeff. That's great stuff!"

"Great? Aren't you exaggerating a bit?" He's still thinking how to change the thought he failed at his action step.

"Not at all! When we aren't aware of our wins, and when we don't take the time to be introspective about what we learn about ourselves, we stay stuck in the same old habits and patterns. We don't move forward . . . How'd the locus of control assessment go?" she asks.

"It went pretty well, I suppose," Jeff says. "I emailed you my results. You tell me, how'd I do?"

Amy puts on a pair of bright red readers and pulls out her notebook. "Hmmm, let's see," she says as she sips her Americano.

"Oh, come on teacher, don't leave me hanging," Jeff says with a smirk and a hint of desperation.

"First of all, it's important to understand, with this and any other assessment, it's not a question of doing well or not doing well. It's all a matter of awareness. Once you're aware of something, especially something like your perspective on things, whether it be locus of control or anything else for that matter, you're on the path to improvement."

Jeff continues to look on intently and a bit impatiently.

"Do you believe that, Jeff?" Amy asks.

"Honestly, I'm not sure I do, Amy," Jeff responds.

"Tell me more . . ." Amy once again prompts.

"Well, listen, I'm a litigator," he begins. "And you know litigation is viewed as a zero-sum game. Close only counts in Scrabble and bocce ball. That's how I view many assessments. I either perform better than the general population or the population I'm competing against, which in this case are other lawyers, or I don't. Pretty simple, actually," he concludes.

"I get it, Jeff," Amy says. "We litigators are a unique breed. It's a big concept, but it's an important one." She sips her coffee. "Okay, on your assessment, with a scale of zero to twelve, you scored right in the middle at a six. That means you have some work to do in the area, and you don't have a predominant frame of mind either way. What this tells me is you may have an external locus of control in some matters, an internal one on others. Does that sound about right to you?"

Jeff ponders for a moment or two. "I suppose."

"Can you give me an example of an area where you have an external locus of control?" Amy asks.

Jeff considers the question. "Of course I can. I cannot control when clients call me. As their lawyer, I have to be available to them. In fact, before my admin, Pam, chastised me for doing so, I would give clients my cell number so they could reach me 24/7."

Amy stops eating her avocado toast mid bite. "You what?!" she exclaims.

The forcefulness of Amy's response takes Jeff aback. He was about to sip his coffee but, instead, puts his cup down and stares at Amy.

Amy takes a deep breath before continuing. "Oh, no, no, no, *no*, Jeff. That is one of the biggest mistakes you can make." She sets her toast down and takes another deep breath. "Of course, you're not alone, I see lawyers make that error all the time. It's based on one of The 5 Lies we lawyers have agreed to. It's those five lies which have, in my view, resulted in the law going from a noble profession to lawyers being a punch line."

"You're pretty passionate about this Amy. What gives?" Jeff asks.

"Remember back when we were having lunch at the CLE in Irvine and I told you I believe the law is a noble profession?" Amy asks.

"Of course I do," Jeff responds. "I hadn't heard anyone talk like that in a long time . . . if ever."

"Right. Well, I do talk that way, because it's how I feel. And if I'm not passionate about it, things won't change! The statistics show lawyers are generally miserable. You know the statistics I'm talking about, right?"

"I think I do," Jeff says. "The statistics about self-medicating with alcohol and other substances, depression, anxiety, isolation, not to mention the average length of careers in law. Are those the statistics you're talking about?"

"Yes. And I believe in my soul The 5 Lies are at the root of all the studies showing horrible attorney satisfaction and dreadful burnout."

"So what are The 5 Lies?" Jeff asks as he breaks off a piece of muffin and pops it into his mouth.

"Let's start with lie number three because that's the lie you just told me," she begins. "Lie number three is: 'I have to be available 24/7 for our clients.'"

"Well, don't we?" Jeff asks. "Don't the fees we charge entitle our clients to that kind of access?"

"*Entitle* is an interesting word to use," she observes. "Tell me more."

"Well, it's common sense, Amy. Clients pay lawyers like you and me a handsome rate. Doesn't that entitle them to, among our outstanding legal work, unlimited access to us when they please?"

"What I hear you saying is the better we get at our jobs, and the more we charge our clients, the more access it entitles clients to." Amy's hands are resting in her lap.

"I think that's right," Jeff responds.

"*Absolutely not!*" Amy exclaims, then takes three deep breaths. "You know who has access to me 24/7, Jeff? My husband and my two kids. That's it."

"Has it always been like that?" Jeff asks.

Amy doesn't hesitate. "Nope. Perhaps that's why I'm so passionate about this now. I was where you are and it was a recipe for failure and burnout." She pauses. "Also, it shows the head trash we have around our value and self-worth, but that's for another time."

"Head trash is a term I've never heard before. What does it mean?"

"It's shorthand for our gremlins, assumptions, inferences, and limiting beliefs. Those are our"—she forms air quotes—"GAILs." Amy continues. "Head trash is the ways we get in our own damn way. It prevents us from achieving our full potential as lawyers and human beings. It's also the negative self-talk we hear in our heads."

"I get the burnout part. If my clients are calling me in the evenings, I'm really never able to turn things off. I've got a question, though. How in the world is being available for clients 24/7 a recipe for failure?"

"Look at it this way, Jeff," Amy says. "What will the client remember with that system?" She takes a bite of her avocado toast and lets the question sit.

"I'm not sure I understand," Jeff says, genuinely confused.

"Let me ask it a different way," Amy offers. "Will a client remember when they called and you picked up, or are they more likely to remember that one time you didn't? Will they remember when you returned their text or emailed immediately, or will they remember that time you didn't?"

"Okay, right. My assistant said the same thing. They're much more likely to remember the one time I didn't pick up or take their call or immediately return their text or email," Jeff admits.

"Right! You could be responsive 99.9999 percent of the time, and add as many 9s as you like, but that one time you're not is the time they'll remember," she says. "Setting the expectation you'll be available 24/7 for clients is a recipe for failure. You can't achieve that goal, it is physically impossible. You're not being a hero to your client by allowing them to contact you directly 24/7. Instead, you're setting yourself up to fail."

"You're right, of course," Jeff says. "I can actually think of several times I didn't answer the phone or respond to a client email immediately, and they were upset with me. It felt like the right thing to do in a saturated market." Jeff pauses for a moment. "In fact, do you remember my win from last month? It was not losing my cool when I was confronted by our chief human resources officer. He was upset I didn't return his email right away." He thinks: *Does an internal culture of unlimited availability lead to a perception of failure?*

"That's the whole problem!" Amy exclaims. "That 'differentiator' perspective is at the root of the lie of needing to be available 24/7!" she continues. "Think of it this way, do you have your doctor's cell number?"

"Well, no," Jeff says. "But that's different."

"How so, Jeff? How is that different?" Amy counters.

"Well . . ." Jeff looks down at the floor. "I'm not sure, but I know it is," he concludes.

"Why?" Amy prods. "Because they're busy with other patients? Because their time is valuable? Because they need to have good boundaries so they can concentrate? Because—"

Jeff interrupts. "I see what you're doing here, Amy. Sure, those things are true for me as well, but it *feels* different, you know?" he says pleadingly.

She sips her coffee and lets the silence stretch out. "Jeff, feelings aren't reality. They are the result of a story we tell ourselves." She shifts in her seat, rests her elbows on the table, folds her hands together below her chin, and leans forward. "What you're *really* saying is your time isn't as valuable as your doc's." She looks him straight in the eye. "That's a bunch of malarkey."

"Come on, Amy," Jeff responds. "I'm not saving anyone's life with the legal work I'm doing! Aren't you overstating the comparison a tad?" He beams, trying to return some levity to the conversation.

"I suppose this is why I'm not as good at these conversations as Jessie is," she admits. "I still get sucked into the story instead of remaining detached . . . Would you agree the work you do for your clients is extremely valuable to them?"

"Sure, otherwise they wouldn't hire me or my firm," Jeff concedes.

"Do you know any doctors, Jeff?" Amy continues. "I mean, personally?"

"Sure," Jeff responds. "I know quite a few."

"Go ahead and ask them if they hand out their cell numbers to patients," Amy prods.

"No way!" Jeff exclaims. "They'd wonder why I was asking. Then I'd have to tell them I did it," he says, "and they'd laugh at me!"

"They may, perhaps, laugh at you, Jeff," Amy says, "but ask them anyway. Can that be an action step for you?"

Jeff sighs. "Okay," he says unenthusiastically. He's thinking of his friend Ann, who owns a family practice with two other physicians. Her model is direct primary care, and she doesn't take insurance; it's a cash-only business. She's the one who is probably as close to Jeff in terms of a business model. *She's also the one most likely to fall down on the floor laughing at me when I ask her whether she hands out her cell number.* These thoughts flash across Jeff's mind in nanoseconds.

"Great! Now, let's make it a measurable action step."

Jeff looks at Amy for a moment. "Okay, I'll reach out to three docs I know by the end of the week and ask them."

"Do you have an idea of who those folks are?" Amy asks.

"Yep, I can picture them right now," Jeff says. "I'll make a note in my phone right now and list them."

"Great!" she affirms. "You know, there's another reason being available 24/7 is a recipe for failure. It leads to distracted work where you're not at your best."

"What do you mean?" Jeff asks.

"According to a study from, I think UC Irvine, it takes an average of twenty-three minutes and fifteen seconds to get back on task when you're distracted from doing deep work."[5] She pauses for effect. "Twenty-three minutes! There's also information out of Kings College that the distractions from constant emails, phone, and text messages may temporarily drop your IQ by ten points."[6]

"Wait, what?" Jeff exclaims. "We get dumber when we're interrupted?" Jeff is thinking of his typical day and how often he's interrupted when he's doing deep work. He feels a bit queasy thinking about it.

"That's right," Amy says. "When you're doing deep work and you choose to allow yourself to be interrupted by an email 'ding' or a phone call, even if it is for as little as one minute, it will take you about twenty-three minutes to get back to a state of deep concentration where you were when you were interrupted," Amy confirms. "As a lawyer, one of, if not the, most important things you'll do every day of your professional career is use your brain. Constant interruptions are time killers, for sure."

"So, you're telling me that every time I get interrupted from deep work, it takes me twenty-three minutes to get back to the mental space I was in?" Jeff asks, somewhat bewildered. "That can't possibly be," he says.

"It can't be because it doesn't *feel* true?" she asks.

---

5 Kermit Pattison, "Worker, Interrupted: The Cost of Task Switching," *Fast Company*, July 28, 2008, https://www.fastcompany.com/944128/worker-interrupted-cost-task-switching.

6 Martin Wainwright, "Emails 'pose threat to IQ'," *The Guardian*, April 22, 2005, https://www.theguardian.com/technology/2005/apr/22/money.workandcareers.

"Yes. That's exactly right. It doesn't feel true," Jeff says as he sips his coffee.

"Remember what I said about feelings? They're the result of the story we tell ourselves," Amy reminds him. "Is the story you're telling yourself that, if the science is correct, you've been wasting so much damn time it kills you?"

"That certainly seems like what I'm thinking," Jeff agrees. "I don't want to admit it, but you may be correct."

"Feelings aside for a moment, the science tells us being available for your clients, or your partners, associates, staff, anyone really, at any moment, whether it be an in-person interruption, a phone call, text, or email, absolutely kills your ability to focus."

Jeff considers for a beat. "I know I'm not that great at math, but that's roughly one hour for every three interruptions."

"I know, right?! It's absolutely bonkers when you become aware of it. I mean, how many times are you interrupted during an ordinary workday, Jeff?" Amy asks. "Whether it's others interrupting your deep work, or your brain being distracted by that 'ding' from an email or a text message that you can't seem to ignore?"

"Too many to count!" Jeff exclaims honestly. *Twenty-three minutes per interruption.* He's so fearful of doing the math he doesn't even try.

"I figured," Amy says. "It's totally understandable and, I'm sorry to say, totally normal in our industry. Jeff, my friend, you are not a unicorn when it comes to distractions."

"But the time wasted . . ." Jeff trails off.

"It's a thing to be aware of for sure. But let's put a pin in the distraction costs for another day," Amy says as she looks at her watch. "Are you curious about the other lies we lawyers have bought into?"

"Honestly, I'm afraid!" Jeff says with a grin. "I'm not sure I can handle it."

"As I've said before, awareness is the first step here, mi amigo. Let's rip that Band-Aid off!" Amy grins. "Here are the other lies our band of high-performing, highly intelligent, and misguided brothers and sisters have bought into." She ticks the lies off on the fingers of her left hand beginning with her thumb. "The first lie is you have to grind all the time to be successful." Her index finger is next. "The second, if you're not busy, you're lazy." She pauses and raises her middle finger. "The third, the one we've just talked about, you have to be available 24/7." It's her ring finger's turn. "The fourth lie we have agreed to is money will make you happy." Amy unfolds her pinky and raises it. "And, finally, fifth, asking for help is weakness." She pauses to look at Jeff, her left arm resting on the table, with the fingers and thumb outstretched.

Jeff's gaze shifts from Amy's hand, to Amy, back to her hand, and finally, back at Amy again. He's more than a bit uncomfortable because he believes Amy's got it all wrong. "Well, I'll tell you this," Jeff begins, "I don't believe those things are lies, well, except *maybe* for lie number three, the available 24/7 one. That one I'm beginning to question the validity of."

Amy chuckles and drops her hand. "Of course you don't, Jeff," she says knowingly. "You've been bamboozled by those who've come before you and those around you. You've succumbed to group think of the worst kind." Amy shakes her head. "I know because I was right where you are once! My head trash told me all five were true."

"Hmph. Well, convince me the things you claim are lies aren't true," Jeff challenges. He feels he's in combat now, for his life. If these are all lies, how has that affected his behavior for the past twenty-plus years? *I've wasted so much damn time.*

"Whoa," Amy proclaims, "I'm not in the business of convincing you of anything. You're not a juror or a judge in a case I have. You're a fellow traveler in the law. You're completely autonomous; you believe what you want. I'm simply proposing alternative thoughts, suggesting that some of the things you believe, like The 5 Lies, don't serve you, your clients, firm, family, or community."

Jeff decides to open up and share what he's thinking. "I guess," he says, "I got defensive because what you're saying goes to some of the foundational thoughts I have on a daily basis." Jeff looks at Amy. "If those thoughts are lies, well . . ."

"If those things are lies, what have I been doing all this time?" Amy finishes for him.

"Exactly," Jeff laments.

"Why don't we do this," Amy says. "Let's go through each of the other five lies and talk about them one at a time. I understand hearing them all at once may have been a bit of a, well, shock to your system." She pauses. "Let's unpack them one at a time and see what you think?"

After a deep breath, Jeff agrees. "Okay, let's go." Although he agrees to the exercise, Jeff is a ball of nerves inside. If he were to stop and observe himself he'd understand his sympathetic nervous system, his fight-or-flight reaction, has been triggered. He'd also understand that once that system is engaged, his brain treats it as a life-and-death situation, regardless of the fact he's in a coffee shop in Encinitas, California, and is about as far away from a life-or-death situation as he could imagine. He'd also understand the consequences to his executive functioning in this state; it is trash.

"Lie number one is you have to grind all the time to be successful," Amy begins. "You said this was true, Jeff. What does grinding mean to you?" she asks.

"Well . . ." Jeff looks at the window as he chews a bit of his muffin. "Grinding means head down, working all the time. It means no dead time in my schedule because dead time isn't billable. It means working hard."

"Good enough definition for me . . . What about outside of work?" she asks.

He pauses for two beats, digging down. "I suppose I'm the same outside of work as I am in it," he says. "I'm constantly doing things. I find it hard to stop. Of course, I also do legal work in my off hours." He grimaces.

She looks at him seriously. "Damn, that sucks, Jeff. I'm certain that's not the life you dreamt of having when you went to law school, am I right?"

"Of course you're right, on both fronts. If I had dreamt the life I'd lead wouldn't allow me to leave work at work, at least some of the time, I'd likely never have become an attorney. I sometimes wonder if it's worth it."

"Understood; I've been there," she says. "Let me ask you this, what's the result of grinding, as you've described?"

"That's easy," Jeff says. "Billable hours met, client work accomplished, bonuses achieved."

"Sure, those are the obvious results you want to believe come only from grinding."

"I *want* to believe?" Jeff interjects. "Aren't those the most important results?"

"I suppose, Jeff, it depends on how you define success and whether grinding is necessary to achieve it."

Jeff considers that statement. He certainly hadn't been feeling successful in some of the ways most important to him. That didn't mean, though, he didn't still care about the other ways, the more traditional ways too. "If I don't grind . . ." He trails off again.

"According to how you keep score, I mean, maybe," she begins. "My question is this: If your head is down all the time grinding, when do you invest time in strategic thinking? When do you have the time to step off the hamster wheel and look at the entire field you're playing on, including your outside-of-work life?"

"A hamster wheel," Jeff says. "That's exactly what it feels like sometimes. Strike that, that's what it feels like all the time!" The tension he feels in his gut seems to be easing, the knot loosening a bit. *It's nice to be able to talk about this stuff with someone who I know understands what it's like.*

"Right," Amy responds knowingly. "I know. I get it. I felt the same with Jessie." She pauses. "I'm curious, does it feel like you're on the hamster wheel now?"

"Of course not. But this is *different*." He picks up his coffee and wonders why he doesn't feel like he's on the hamster wheel at the moment.

"Is it?" she asks. "Let's go a bit further. You've mentioned the first level consequences you see in grinding, making billable hours and such. What's the lost opportunity cost of not stepping off the wheel for a bit? What's the strategic cost to you of always being on the hamster wheel?"

"The strategic cost?" Jeff responds. "I'm not sure what you mean. As a firm, the management team plans strategy for the firm annually."

"Let me guess," Amy says, "you talk about marketing, building the firm, cost control, talent acquisition and retention, things like that?"

"Yes," Jeff says. *Where's she going with this?* he wonders.

"That's all well and good, Jeff," Amy continues. "I'm not saying that's not important to the health and well-being of your law firm, because it is."

"Whew," Jeff giggles.

"But that annual planning for the law firm isn't what I'm talking about. I'm talking about *your* strategic time, for *your* law practice and, frankly, for *your* life. What's lost by not doing *that* work?" She takes a bite of toast and lets the question linger.

Finally, Jeff admits, "I'm not sure I understand."

"Strategic thinking requires some foundational things," Amy says. "First and foremost, it requires you to have a target, or a goal. I'm not talking about the billable hour goal here, I'm talking about a goal you set so that your law practice fulfills your purpose."

"My purpose?" Jeff scoffs. "What does fulfilling my purpose have to do with the firm's overall health and well-being?" Now he's quite confused; it feels like they're back in woo-woo land again.

"Jeff, if you're not fulfilling your purpose," Amy says seriously, "what's the damn point of it all?"

"I've never thought about having a law practice that fulfilled my purpose," Jeff says honestly, looking out the window.

"That's normal," Amy responds. "It's not something most lawyers consider when building their practice. Some of us stumble into an area of law we're good at. Others of us have an area of law thrust upon us because the firm needs someone, anyone, to become the go-to in that area and the powers that be pick someone for the work. Few of us are intentional about either choosing a practice area, or shaping one that is thrust upon us, in a way that fulfills our purpose." She pauses and sips her coffee. "Now let's talk about your definition of success," Amy continues.

"Success for a lawyer is billable hours and bonuses. If you're in a firm like mine, or, presumably, yours Amy, it's about climbing the ladder and making partner. If you're a solo, it's getting a sufficient number of clients so you don't worry so much about where the next one will come from." Jeff says. "Obviously!" He believes the answer is so self-evident as to make the question itself nonsensical. The answer comes so naturally, he doesn't even have to think about it. When he pauses for a moment to do so, though, he thinks, *Hitting those things hasn't made me a success in my mind, though, has it?*

"If you think those are the definitions of success for lawyers, sure," Amy says with a hint of challenge.

"That's how we keep score in our industry, Amy. Billable hours, bonuses, and the like. That's what separates the winners from the losers." Even as the words leave his mouth, though, he wonders, *But is that the right way to keep score?*

"Let me ask you this question," Amy says, still serious. "What do you want your legacy to be?"

Jeff is confused by the pivot. "What do you mean?" he asks.

"What's the one word or phrase you want people to utter about you at your memorial service after your race is run?" Amy clarifies. She waits patiently for the answer.

It's Jeff's turn to grow serious, "I've never really thought of that. Give me a moment." He looks out the garage-door windows.

"Take all the time you need," Amy says.

"I suppose I'd want the word to be 'kind,'" Jeff says. "Yes, that's it, 'kind.'" He's not certain what his legacy has to do with success in his law practice, but he's willing to play along.

"Here's how someone once described the difference between the kind of legacy we're talking about and the type of legacy people normally default to," Amy says. "You can bequeath to the people you leave behind your worldly goods, you know, like property and such."

Jeff nods his head.

"It is impossible for you, in your Last Will and Testament, to bequeath how you made a person feel. Your will can't say 'I leave to my wife the feeling she had when I surprised her with . . .' You can fill in the blank." She pauses to let her words sink in. "If your desired legacy is that you were kind," Amy says, "that's your definition of success. Now, tell me what making your billable hour requirements and earning bonuses and, for that matter making partner, have to do with that word," she challenges.

Jeff doesn't miss a beat, "Well, honestly, not much." He feels something open up as he responds. *Am I beginning to understand?* he wonders.

"That's a knee-jerk lazy reaction, Jeff. Think about it some more," Amy replies. "We're not here to play on the surface. We're here to go deep, perhaps deeper than you've ever gone."

Jeff stares out the window at traffic going by on the 101. "Well, I guess it depends on how I go about making my billable hour requirement. If I'm kind to staff and understanding with clients, that could demonstrate kindness," he admits.

"On the other hand?" Amy prompts.

"On the other hand, if I'm an ogre, like some partners I've worked with, that would be antithetical to being remembered as being kind," Jeff concludes.

"So, what I'm hearing you say is that although hitting the billable hour target isn't kind in and of itself, it can be done in a kind way. That will result in people remembering you the way you want to be remembered?" Amy asks.

"I suppose that's right. It's not hitting the target, but how I go about doing so," Jeff says.

"Okay," Amy continues. "Do you still think lie number one is true? Remember, the first lie is you have to grind all the time to be successful." She shifts and sips her coffee.

"It's that word 'grind' that's now got me hung up. It seems to me that grinding will naturally result in me being less kind," Jeff says.

"Interesting," Amy says. "Let's dig a bit deeper. Can you grind and be kind, or will grinding result in you being different than you'd otherwise want to be?" she asks.

"That's a deep question," Jeff says as he takes out his phone. "Don't worry, I'm just making a note of the question I have for myself."

"I figured," Amy replies. "Care to share the question?"

"It's not fully formed," Jeff admits. "I'm not ready to share it."

"All good," she says good-naturedly and glances at her watch. "I think we'll be able to get to one more lie today and will have to pick up the rest next time," Amy says. "Are you good with that?"

"Of course!" Jeff exclaims. "I've got to get to the office relatively soon anyway."

"Lie number two is the belief that if you're not busy, you're lazy," Amy reminds him. "Does that land at all?" She takes the final bite of her avocado toast.

"I'm not sure," Jeff says candidly. "Can you explain a bit more?"

"Sure. I'll give you an example from my life," Amy offers. "Back before I began working with Jessie, I felt this overwhelming, I guess the word is *need*, to not have any blank spots on my calendar. Any time there was a blank spot, I was compelled to have my assistant Anna Maria 'fill' it."

"I can relate," Jeff says.

"I mean, it was a visceral feeling, almost like nausea, you know?" Amy asks as she looks past Jeff at the shelves opposite them.

Jeff decides to be real, honest, and more open in this moment. "I do!" he says. "100 percent!"

"Tell me," Amy encourages as she finishes off her coffee.

"It seems tied to your lie number one," Jeff begins. "It's part and parcel of the same type of perspective. Anyway, if I see any, and I mean *any*, blank space on my calendar, I feel guilty and either ask Pam to fill it, or I fill it myself, which, she'll tell you, is a terrible idea."

"You used a powerful word there, Jeff, 'guilty.' Why is that?" Amy asks. "What's up with the guilt?"

"I think that feeling was instilled in me from the time I was a baby lawyer, you know?" Jeff asks.

"I certainly do," Amy responds.

"Anyway," Jeff says. He waves his hands in an "it is what it is" gesture.

"What if I told you that lie gets it exactly backward?" Amy asks. "What I mean is, I believe if you're busy, you're lazy."

"Look, Amy, I'm willing to have an open mind here, but you're not making a lick of sense right now," Jeff challenges. "If I'm busy how can I possibly be lazy?" he asks, a bit exasperated. "Have we entered the 'Upside Down'?"

"Ha!" Amy exclaims. "I love the *Stranger Things* reference, my friend, but, no, we're not in the Upside Down. Nor are we playing the 'opposite game' I used to play with my kids," she continues.

"Emma and I used to play that game as well," Jeff says, smiling.

"I mean it. If you're busy, you're lazy. Allow me to explain," she says. "If you're busy, you're not making the tough decisions about what should and should not be on your calendar. You're doing too much and often too much of the stuff you ought not be doing."

"How do you mean?" Jeff asks.

"Jeff, you're the managing partner at a world-class midsized law firm, right?" Amy asks.

"Damn right." Jeff crows as he sits a bit taller and puffs his chest out a bit.

"If we were to look at your calendar for the week, how many things are there on it you should not be doing?"

"Oh, some, but not that many," Jeff responds.

"Really? Are you sure?" Amy presses knowingly.

"Pretty sure," Jeff says in a most unsure tone.

"Don't BS me," Amy chides. "You're not sure at all and that's okay."

Jeff doesn't respond. *She's right, I've got no idea.*

"Do you know what Steve Jobs had to say about focus?" Amy asks.

"Nope," he admits.

"At some Apple event or another, Jobs said something like, 'Focusing is about saying no. You've got to say no, no, no, and when you say no, you piss off people.'"[7] Amy pauses to allow it to sink in. After a beat, she continues, "I'm going to issue you a challenge, Jeff. I did this challenge with Jessie, my coach, way back at the beginning stages of our relationship . . . here's what I want you to do: Pick a charity or individual you would rather die than give money to. I mean die. Don't tell me what or who it is; I don't care. Got it?"

"Yep, sure do," Jeff responds.

"Great! Now, what's your real hourly rate?" Amy asks.

"I bill at $995 per hour," Jeff responds sheepishly.

"First, you're not charging enough!" Amy says. "But that's not the point of what we're doing here. That's your billable rate. What's your time actually worth?" she continues.

"I'm not sure what you mean," Jeff says.

"Okay. Let's go about it this way. Back when your daughter Emma was born, do you remember that time?" Amy asks.

"Of course I do. I can see us at Scripps Mary Birch Hospital right now if I close my eyes," Jeff says. "You know I held Emma even before Jen did. Mom was struggling with the anesthesia from her C-section." He beams at the memory.

"That's great. Now, how much would someone, anyone, have had to pay you to not be at your daughter's birth?" she asks.

Jeff thinks hard for a moment before responding. "I don't

---

7   Zameena Mejia, "Steve Jobs: Here's What Most People Get Wrong About Focus," CNBC Make It, October 2, 2018, https://tinyurl.com/5n7v87j5.

know if there's an amount of money in the world anyone could have paid me to miss Emma's birth."

Amy grins. "I had the same response when Jessie asked me the question. But dig deeper. I bet there is, in fact, a dollar amount. So, what is it?"

Jeff sits with the question. "I honestly don't know." He's struggling. "Is there an amount of money anyone could have paid me *before* I'd had the experience? Probably," he admits to himself, a bit shamefully. "But having experienced the event, I know there really ought not have been."

"Okay, that question may be too big," Amy admits. "How about this one. How much should a client pay you to miss Emma's next basketball game?"

"Ouch!" Jeff exclaims, recalling the last missed game and his conversation with Emma.

"Look, this is all about getting real, Jeff," Amy says. "You missed one recently and felt guilty. That's when you were billing at $995 an hour, right?" Amy asks.

"Yes," he admits.

"Is that still the number someone would have to pay you to miss the next game you promise her you'd be at? Put another way, what would someone have to pay you so when you did the analysis, you would decide the money was worth it?" Amy continues to probe.

"Okay. I'll say $5,000 per hour," Jeff responds.

"Great, that's still too low, but will work for our purposes. That's your hourly rate for this experiment," Amy continues. "Now, keep track of all the things you ought not be doing as the managing partner of a world-class midsized law firm. I know you're good at tracking your time, aren't you?" Amy says.

"That I am," Jeff responds. "Aren't all lawyers?"

They both laugh good-naturedly.

Amy continues. "Keep track of your time spent on these things like any good attorney. At the end of each week, total the time up, then multiply it by $5,000 per hour to get the value of your time, which is essentially wasted. Write a check in that amount to the entity or person you have in mind—the one you'd rather die than give a cent to."

"Whoa, Amy! I'm not comfortable sending that money out!" Jeff says.

"Easy there, Jeff. You don't have to actually send the money!" Amy says. "But tracking your time and writing the check will make it more real for you." She pauses. "Put the checks in the drawer, and at the end of four weeks, add them up. Even better, bring them to our next meeting. You'll see how much time you've spent on things you ought not be doing."

"I feel better about this exercise already," Jeff says with a sigh of relief. "But can't I just track the time? Why do I have to put a dollar amount on it?"

"Time is such a tough concept for our brains to deal with," Amy says. "Look at any outstanding personal injury lawyer who can turn something as amorphous as 'pain and suffering' into something understandable to a jury. They put a dollar amount on it because humans understand the value of money. We do not understand the value of our time."

"Gotcha. Okay. I'll do the exercise, but I'm certain the dollar amount won't be all that much."

"We'll see, won't we," Amy says through a Cheshire cat grin. "Remember, what's measured can be improved, so we shall see."

Amy stands up. "Time to go, Jeff. For our next session, how does four weeks from today work for you?"

"Four weeks from today," Jeff confirms. "Looks great!"

"We'll see how much money you'd be paying your least favorite organization or person. We'll also go over the remainder of The 5 Lies. Do you have them in mind?"

"Can you remind me again?" Jeff asks as he pulls up his phone's Notes app.

"Absolutely!" she says enthusiastically, and gives him a moment to get his phone ready to take notes. "Lie number one. You have to grind all the time to be successful. Lie number two. If you're not busy, you're lazy. Lie number three. You have to be available 24/7. Lie number four. Money will make you happy. Lie number five. Asking for help is weakness."

"Got 'em!" He gathers his and Amy's trash to toss on the way out.

"Okay, see you four weeks from today. Same bat time, same bat channel."

"See you then."

As Jeff and Amy head to the door, Amy catches Molly's attention. "See you soon, Molly!"

She looks up from the pastry case. "Yes you will! Will I see Jeff in about four weeks?" Molly asks.

Jeff looks at Amy. "How does she know we'll meet in four weeks?"

"Not important, Jeff," Amy responds and looks at Molly. "That's right, but you'll see me sooner!"

"Looking forward to it!" Molly says. Without missing a beat, she announces, "Espresso for John!"

Amy and Jeff walk out of Better Buzz. "Don't forget your homework! Track that time and write those checks!"

"Will do!" Jeff tosses back. *Even if they won't be for that much money.*

As Jeff speeds down the 5 heading for his office, he considers how he'll tackle this new action step. *First, I suppose I'll have to decide what work I ought to be doing. That would seem to make the most sense.*

He comes up with his touchstone. *I only ought to be doing work absolutely no one else at the firm can do, and that work must require someone with my training and expertise.*

As he pulls into the parking deck, he's got his plan. He's decided the things he ought to be doing are high-level legal work for his clients, creating high-value clients for the firm, and presiding over meetings where he's indispensable. He'll track his time as he normally does, in real time—a task he's good at—and wait until the end of the week to review and tally it. *What would be the fun in editing what I'm doing beforehand? That won't give me a true picture. Plus, I'm really not concerned.* "I think Amy's going to be surprised," he crows as he nears the elevator.

When he arrives home that evening a bit later than he'd hoped, Jeff shares with Jen the exercise he'll be doing over the next four weeks. "Interesting," she says. "I sure am glad you don't have to mail the checks you'll be writing!" she exclaims as she kisses him. "We'd be broke."

"Hey," Jeff replies. "Do you think I do much work I shouldn't be doing?" The confidence he felt when Amy made the challenge to him this morning was fading.

"It really doesn't matter what I think, honey," Jen says kindly in an attempt to escape answering Jeff's question. "The math will tell the story." She gets the air fryer out of the cupboard. "Burgers and fries tonight, okay? Oh, before I forget, I've invited Tony and Ann over for dinner Saturday. Cool?"

"Yes to burgers and fries," Jeff says, "and yes to dinner with Tony and Ann. It's been too long." *And I've got a question for Ann about whether she gives patients her cell number.*

Beliefs Built on Lies

THE NEXT WEEK passes by in a blur. Jeff has what he considers to be a "normal" week, nothing really out of the ordinary. He hits his target of thirty-five billable hours for the week, presides over or attends four meetings, and does the normal, day-to-day things attorneys do. When Friday afternoon hits, he's sitting at his desk with his time report in front of him. He's also got the electronic note listing his "ought to be doing" list open on his computer.

"Let's go!" he says enthusiastically. He's looking forward to this.

As he goes down his time report, he highlights the items not on his "ought to do" list with a yellow highlighter. Such things include administrative tasks others at GH&B are more than capable of doing, routine discovery responses and other low-hanging legal work, and client interactions that could have been delegated.

As he moves down the page, he's struck by how much yellow there is. *That must have just been a bad day.* He flips the page and continues the exercise. By the time he gets to the end of his time he's highlighted more than he feels comfortable with. "What the hell?" he says aloud. "Ten hours? How can that be?" Jeff sits in silence for a moment in disbelief. "Ten hours? That cannot be right." He goes back to the first page and does his analysis again. To his dismay, he's identified an additional .8 hours of work that didn't make his original highlights. "Well," he says as he picks his head up from the paper, "the numbers don't lie, my friend. I didn't even include the meetings I didn't have to be at in the total."

He gets out his checkbook and pens a check for $54,000.00. His hand actually shakes a bit as he writes the name of the person on the "Pay to the order of" line. "I've got to do better next week or I may have a heart attack," he says as he gathers his things and gets ready to head home.

When he arrives home, Jen is on the patio reading. He walks over, kisses her on the cheek, and asks the standard question he's asked seemingly every day since they met. "How was your day?" he says, and sits down on the outdoor couch next to her.

"Oh, my day was great," she says. "How was yours?"

"Same as always," he replies.

Jen drops her readers down her nose and gives Jeff a questioning look.

"What?" he asks, a bit bewildered.

"How'd your action step go?" she asks. "Weren't you going to total up the hours you spent on stuff you ought not be doing? I've been waiting all day to find out the answer!" she says with more glee than Jeff feels is warranted.

He looks at her with a bit of sadness in his eyes. "It's worse than I imagined. I wasted more than ten hours this week," he says. "And this felt like a relatively normal week. That means if we extrapolate it out, I'm wasting more than five hundred hours in a year." He sits quietly for a moment letting that number sink in, not for Jen but for himself.

"Don't be too hard on yourself, honey," she says. "Knowledge is power, right?"

He finishes her statement. "Only if I actually do something about it!"

THE NEXT THREE weeks fly by for Jeff, filled with legal work, administrative tasks, and family obligations. On Friday of each week, though, he invests time in the action step he's committed to, totaling the time he's spent on things he "ought not to," and writing what he now considers "that damn check." On the final Friday before his next meeting with Amy, he writes the last check and totals the amounts—$178,000.00.

It's definitely not what he expected to report back.

Chapter 5

More Lies

"All persons ought to endeavor to follow what is right, and not what is established."

~ ARISTOTLE

The next Monday at Better Buzz, it's a gloomy coastal San Diego morning. It's cool by San Diego standards; the garage-door windows at the coffee shop are closed. Amy is sitting at her regular table, thankful she surfed yesterday. This morning was so dreary she went for a run instead.

Now she's looking forward to finding out the results of Jeff's homework assignment. She is certain—if he was honest—he'll be surprised at the amount of time he spends doing stuff he shouldn't be doing. Her certainty comes from years of experience; not only has she done the exercise on a fairly regular basis, but she's also had partners and associates in her firm do the same.

JEFF LEAVES THE house a bit later than he'd hoped, again. As he drives down the 5 nearing Encinitas, he pictures the checks he'll show Amy. He's embarrassed.

At his true hourly rate, the value of his time spent on things he shouldn't be doing as a managing partner was shocking. He tried to convince himself the month was an anomaly, but he knows that's a lie. The four weeks were typical. *It's no wonder I don't have time for the important stuff. I'm wasting so much freaking time doing things I didn't go to law school to do!*

Jeff parks his car on D street and notices he's parked right behind Amy. *How in the world does she always get here before me?* he wonders as he jogs south on the 101 in the direction of Better Buzz.

Amy stands up to meet him in line once he opens the door. "Good morning!" she exclaims cheerfully.

"Good morning! Sorry I'm a bit late," Jeff says.

"Hey, your timing is getting better each time we meet," Amy says seriously. "That's what life is all about, getting a bit better every day."

After they order, Amy and Jeff walk back to their table and sit in their usual seats, and Amy begins their conversation in the usual way. "Tell me about a win!"

This time, Jeff was prepared for this question and proudly says so. "I knew you were going to ask me that, and today, I'm fully prepared to answer. My win has to do with the homework assignment."

Amy looks on intrigued. "Oh, really? Well, spill the beans! Or should I say, 'Show me the money'?"

As Molly calls out their orders, Jeff takes the checks he's written out of his planner and lays them on the table with a smile.

Amy looks down at the checks and mentally totals them in her head. "Interesting. I'll get our stuff." As she walks to the counter, she's wondering why Jeff believes this is a win.

Jeff folds his hands on the table and waits patiently.

Amy returns with coffees and toast, sits down, and begins. "Okay, I'm ready to hear about how this pile of money, which you would be loath to give, is a win." Her tone is curious, non-judgmental, and open.

"Well, as I was driving down here, I felt embarrassed thinking about the amount of money I wasted this past month. I was going to try to explain it away and tell you it wasn't a typical month . . . that would have been a lie, though."

Amy nods her head.

"As I parked my car, it hit me like a lightning bolt." His grin grows larger.

"Go on," Amy says encouragingly, the corners of her mouth beginning to turn up in faint smile.

"My win is knowing. That's it. If I hadn't done the homework and been completely honest with it, to myself and to you, what's the freaking point, you know? We're investing valuable time here during our meetings and I'm doing the work afterward. They say knowledge is power. Now I know, and you were right, the checks made it somehow more real for me. That's my win!"

Amy extends her left hand up in the air, offering it to Jeff. "High-five here, please!" They high-five each other and laugh.

"That, my friend," Amy says gleefully, "is a growth mindset."

They grin at each other.

"What did you learn about yourself?" Amy asks as she takes a bite of her toast.

"Ha! I'm ready for that one as well," Jeff smirks. "I learned I'm much better off knowing, even if the news is bad. Operating with knowledge is much better than simply guessing because that leads to some incorrect assumptions." He sips his coffee, still grinning.

"Tell me more," Amy says.

Jeff is quiet for a moment, giving Amy's request its due. As he considers what to say, he finds the silence comforting. After a minute, he says, "The checks sitting in front of us are a perfect example. When I left our last meeting, I was sure, and I do mean *sure*, I'd be able to prove you wrong and that the amount of time I spent on things I ought not be doing as the managing partner of a world-class midsized law firm was minimal. These checks tell a totally different story."

"Yes, they certainly do, Jeff," she says as she sips her coffee.

"And, without doing the work, I would have simply continued to operate in the dark, assuming I was focused on what I should be focused on. That, Amy, turns out to be a lie. A lie of the most pernicious kind; a lie based on ignorance." He peacefully sits back in his chair, enjoying the coolness of the metal on his back.

Amy looks delighted. "Jeff, that's an important shift. Many of us go through life making assumptions about things, measurable things. We can, of course, measure just about anything; it's a matter of investing the time to do so. It's also a matter of over-coming the fear we feel in actually having data, you know?" She pauses and looks at him. "If we take the time to do the work and gather the data, we no longer have the excuse of ignorance." She leans in. "When we stop and actually measure those things, we often find our assumptions to be wildly incorrect."

Jeff sips his coffee and glances at the infant and mother sitting at the next table. "As you said, investing the time to actually track what I was spending my time on was a bit scary despite my bravado," Jeff admits sheepishly. "It required me to change the way I thought about things and, honestly, I wasn't sure I wanted to peak behind the curtain when it came right down to it. My bluster with you aside, of course," Jeff says.

"Tell me about the change in thinking," Amy prompts, taking another bite of her peanut butter toast.

"Well, first of all, the homework assignment required me to believe certain things I had paid lip service to in the past which may not have been aligned with my actions and mentality," he says.

"Such as?"

"For example, I was embarrassed to say that GH&B is a"—Jeff now makes air quotes—"'world-class midsized law firm.' Did I believe we were good at what we did? Of course. Did I believe we were elite? I'm not so sure." For some reason, this admission isn't difficult to make to Amy.

"Why was it important for you to believe GH&B is a best-in-class law firm for you to do the exercise?" Amy says.

"If I didn't, it would have thrown the whole analysis off!" Jeff exclaims. "If I didn't believe GH&B was top-tier, I could lie to myself about whether I should be doing the tasks I was doing."

"Tell me more," Amy says again, drawing Jeff further down the path.

He pauses, looks out on the foggy Encinitas morning, then turns back to Amy and continues. "If GH&B wasn't world-class, I could convince myself some of the things on the line between doing/not doing would be tipped into the wrong column. If I considered us simply a good law firm, I thought I could do more things that the managing partner of a gold standard law firm ought not be doing."

Amy sips her coffee. "Interesting. How did adopting the belief GH&B is world-class affect your decision-making process?"

"It made the choices I was required to make, I don't know, starker."

"How so?"

"Well," Jeff continues as he leans forward in his chair and folds his hands on the table, "an elite law firm requires its managing partner to set the tone for being world class. Here's an example. When I was doing the assignment, I came to a decision point on a task I would normally not have thought twice about doing, reviewing a client's discovery responses to ensure accuracy. Of course, they have to be reviewed. I'm not suggesting otherwise.

But was I in the best position to review them? Of course not. The associate who was more intimately involved in the matter was in the best position to review the responses and suggest any changes. The more I thought about it, the more I realized the associate would benefit because I would be modeling delegation skills for them. The client would appreciate it because the work wouldn't be billed at my higher rate. I would appreciate it because I would be taking something off my plate. It's a win all around."

"Congratulations on all of this, Jeff," she says. "How can you take what you've learned in the exercise and continue to have that mentality moving forward?"

"It's all about awareness, I suppose. Taking that beat before diving into something and asking whether I'm the one to be doing that thing."

"Awareness is the key," Amy agrees. "Okay, are you ready to dive into the rest of The 5 Lies?" Amy asks.

"You bet!" Jeff says.

"Let's recap," Amy says, "The 5 Lies are . . . number one. You have to grind all the time to be successful. Number two. If you're not busy, you're lazy. Number three. You have to be available 24/7. Number four. Money will make you happy. And number five. Asking for help is weakness. We tackled numbers one and two last time, so let's talk about the rest, starting with number three."

"I've begun to see the light on number three already. It's bullshit, frankly."

"I seem to recall you were supposed to ask three of your doctor friends whether they give out their cell number to their patients as your second action step. That fits squarely into lie three. How'd that go?"

Jeff looks on sheepishly, "Oh, that?" He sips his coffee. "Well, I actually didn't completely blow it off if that matters!"

He flashes back to the last few weeks and that dinner with Tony and Ann. He had remembered to ask her, and her response was no surprise. "I can't say I asked three friends, but we had one doctor friend over to dinner and—well, she actually laughed out loud when I asked." He takes a breath. "The funny thing, Amy, was when the question was coming out of my mouth, it sounded ridiculous, even to me. That's why I didn't ask two more of my doctor friends. I didn't need to. I've got it. The concept of being available 24/7 for clients is a lie. It's nonsense and not a differentiator at all, but an opportunity for failure."

Amy nods her head.

"I agree. Listen, Jeff. Like I said before, the only people on the planet I'm available to 24/7 are my husband and my kids. That's it. Certainly, at the firm, everyone must go through my assistant, Waylon, to get to me. It's his job to determine whether something warrants my personal involvement or if it's better handled by a member of the team. If he makes the decision that I must be involved, he schedules a specific time in my time block dedicated to returning calls, and I make the call."

"Wait, you only return calls at certain times during your day?"

"That's right. I return calls from 3 p.m. to 5 p.m. That's it. I don't spend time on the phone during the day; I've got more important work to do and, typically, phone calls deal with other people's priorities."

"I like that! I'd love to be able to focus only on my priorities for the majority of the day. It may also help me focus on the most important things I do and reduce the gawd awful amount of the checks sitting between us!"

"It's a game changer!" Amy says. "It really is, but let's leave that discussion for another day. It sounds like you've got a good handle on lie number three, do you have any other questions about it?"

"Nope, I'm solid there," he says.

"Good deal. Let's tackle lie number four: money will make you happy. First, let me ask you, on a scale of one to ten, with ten being you absolutely believe money will make you happy and one being you know it can't, where are you?"

"I suppose I'm at a solid five," Jeff says.

Amy sips her coffee. "Explain."

"Well, I'm not a monk and haven't taken a vow of poverty, so, to a certain extent, money is important."

"Right," Amy says. "We've all got mortgages to pay, kids to put through school, maybe even student loans to pay, and so on. I haven't taken a vow of poverty either. So Jeff, do you believe money can make you happy?"

"Sure!"

"That was a quick answer," Amy responds. "Tell me more."

"I'll give you a perfect example. We're about to go on the 'college tour' with our daughter Emma. I am fortunate enough to have made a good living, so we'll be able to have Emma go to the school of her choice without a mountain of debt like my wife and I had when we graduated. And that will make me happy."

"I get it!" Amy says. "We did it a bit differently and made sure our kids had some financial 'skin in the game' when it came to their education, but you're right, being in the position we are in to help our children out does bring us joy."

"That's what I'm talking about," Jeff says. "And on a smaller scale, it makes me happy I'm getting a new longboard from Encinitas Surfboards." He nods his head north in the direction of the surf shop which is up the 101.

"Ah, there's absolutely nothing like a new surfboard to bring a smile to your face," Amy trumpets.

"Right! So, yes, I would say that money can make you happy," Jeff concludes.

"Now, turn that analytical lawyer brain of yours on and think critically about the lie, money will make you happy."

Jeff sips his coffee. "I suppose in my examples it isn't the money that actually makes me happy, it's the things I'm able to do with the money that are the source of my joy."

"That's interesting," Amy says. "Tell me more about your thought process there."

"Give me time to think about this," he asks. He's quiet for a moment and then says, "Well, I suppose if money makes people happy, the people out there in the world with ungodly amounts of money would be the happiest people on the planet."

"Seems logical. Is that true? Are the people who have the most money the happiest?" Amy asks.

"Not from what I read," Jeff chortles. "Sometimes it seems the more money someone has, the sadder they may be."

"Right!" Amy exclaims. "It's like what The Notorious B.I.G. rapped about. 'Mo money mo problems!' . . . So, if some of the wealthiest people in the world aren't happy, can the concept of money making us happy stand up?"

"When you really think about it, no," Jeff answers honestly.

"The other issue," Amy says, "with thinking money makes you happy is the goal posts are constantly moving. We think 'when I make x number of dollars' or 'when I have x dollars in net worth,' I'll be happy. When we get to that number, whatever it is, and we're not as happy as we want to be, we move the finish line to another dollar figure. The cycle is never-ending."

"I can see that being the case. In fact, if I think about it, I've participated in that vicious cycle myself," Jeff says.

"Jeff, I think that's something the vast majority of us do. You aren't a unicorn, my friend." Amy finishes her peanut butter toast with one final bite. "Do you know the five biggest regrets people have on their deathbed?" Amy asks.

"I don't, but I bet you're going to tell me none of them are about money." Jeff titters.

"My, my, you are perceptive! None of them have anything to do with money. Instead, they have to do with living a full and authentic life."

Jeff considers the regrets he'd have if his last moment were tomorrow; money isn't one of them. "Tying your happiness to the amount of money you make or that's in your bank account is a fool's errand, it seems."

"Exactly! Now, again, I'm not saying money doesn't matter; of course it does . . . up to a certain point. After that, it loses its internal value. If you haven't seen this at GH&B with the new generation of attorneys, you soon will." She goes silent and looks out the window thinking of her multigenerational office of high-achieving attorneys. "These 'kids'"—now Amy uses air quotes—"understand happiness is not the result of money, which is why they ask for other forms of compensation like time off, the ability to work remotely, or coaching for self-improvement."

"Now that you mention it, we are seeing that at GH&B. I never tied it to the lie we're talking about." He sips his coffee.

"Not surprising. It all goes back to awareness! Unless you take the time to think about it, you're much more likely to be confused by their request when, in fact, it is an outright acknowledgment of something true. Money does not equate to happiness."

"You're right."

"Now, on to lie number five," Amy says. "Asking for help is weakness. So, on a scale of one to ten, how much do you buy this lie?"

"Before I give you my answer, I need to tell you Jen brought this topic up recently. You and Jen haven't been trading notes, have you?" he snickers.

"Nope. Chalk it up to two great minds thinking alike."

"I guess I'm probably—again—at a five out of ten. I mean, look, I'm the managing partner of a law firm, I'm a lawyer and a litigator. If I show weakness and ask for help too much, other lawyers would be all over it like sharks smelling blood in the water. I know I would. That's the game lawyers play."

"Seems like it, huh?" she agrees. "Let me ask you this. Who's your favorite professional athlete?"

Jeff takes a beat, and another. "I'll say the third baseman for my San Diego baseball team."

"Oh, why did you have to pick a Padre," Amy grimaces. "You know I live in Los Angeles, right?"

"I know, but I meant no offense!" Jeff feigns regret. "Well, perhaps a bit," he grins.

Amy turns serious. "Do you think the third baseman is weak?"

"Of course not, he's a great baseball player."

"How many coaches do you think the third baseman has?"

"Well, he's got the manager of the team, he's got a batting coach, I'd bet he gets coached on fielding, strength and conditioning, nutrition, and maybe even media relations," Jeff says. "If he's smart, and I believe he is, he's also got a team that advises him on his financial affairs."

"That's quite a stable of professionals to help your third baseman," Amy says deadpan.

"But, that's different, he's a professional athlete, not a lawyer!"

Amy shakes her head. "Everyone draws that artificial and, in my opinion, nonsensical distinction." She continues. "How about we do this. Let's, for a moment, step back and look at the similarities between you and your third baseman for a moment. Are you game?"

"Sure, but I'm no professional athlete," Jeff says. "However good I was in Little League."

"In order for this to exercise to have any meaning, could you suspend judgment on that for a moment?" Amy asks.

"I suppose . . ."

"Here's what we know about your third baseman. First, what he does, only a small percentage of the population on the entire planet can do. And, of course, no one does it exactly as he can. Do you agree?"

"Of course! But—"

"Hold right there," Amy interrupts. "You're going to say there are thousands of lawyers who can do what you do, right?"

"Yep."

"What if I told you that was not true and that belief system sells you short on so many levels?" Amy is now as serious as Jeff's ever seen her. "Humor me for a moment here Jeff, will you?" she continues. "Answer me this question. Who on the planet has the exact same experiences you've had? I'm not talking only legal experiences, but life experiences?"

"I don't know how to answer that question, Amy. I mean, the obvious answer is no one."

"Sometimes the obvious answer is the answer, Jeff!" She allows her response to sink in. "What lawyer on the planet uses the same language with their clients, or thinks of things the way you do? I'm not talking in general legal ways, but with all the contours, colors, and nuances you do?"

Jeff contemplates the question, hell-bent on not reacting to it but, instead, giving a thoughtful response. "Because not a single other person in the history of the world has had the same life experiences I've had, the answer to that question is, again, no one else."

"Right! Are you feeling a bit more like a unique 'player'?"

"I suppose," Jeff offers tentatively.

"Great. Now stick with me. Every professional baseball player has had to hone their skills to be elite at their craft, correct?"

"Sure, many of those guys have been playing at an elite level since they've been in junior high school." Jeff feels like he's stating the obvious.

"Do you believe you've honed your skills to be a great lawyer?" Amy challenges.

"I'm not sure about 'great'"—air quotes again—"but darn good, that's for sure."

"Don't be self-effacing here, Jeff. You're the managing partner of an outstanding law firm. There's no way you are in the position you are without being a great lawyer." She looks directly in his eyes. "You're a trial lawyer, so I know you have ego." She smirks. "I know because I do as well."

"I suppose you're right," he says, with a bit more confidence.

"Do you think your third baseman can show weakness? Isn't there always someone younger with as much, if not more, talent waiting for him to show weakness so he can take the starting job?"

"Of course." Jeff nods.

"Your third baseman is rare and unique, just like you. Your third baseman honed his craft to become one of the best on the planet, just like you. If your third baseman shows weakness, there's always someone waiting in the wings to take advantage of that, like you said about the legal profession. What did you call it?"

"Like sharks who smell blood in the water," Jeff replies.

"That's right. Don't you see, Jeff, lawyers have more in common with professional athletes than we see on the surface."

"I guess you're right." Jeff still isn't completely there, but he's much further along in accepting the analogy Amy is drawing than when she began.

"Shift the frame you use to look at yourself and your profession and you'll see it's true." She sips her water. "Because that's true, you can do as your third baseman has and enlist a team of people to help you in a bunch of ways. You already do! You've got Pam, other staff, and associates."

"It would be impossible for me to do my best without them," Jeff agrees.

"Right," Amy says. "Having help outside of the context of your law firm is equally important. My coach has helped me the most with my mindset. I know darn well I wouldn't be where I am today without him. I also know that my family and my community appreciate where I am today . . . I also know if other lawyers buy into the lie asking for help is weakness, I'll be elite, and they will not. It's really that simple."

"I never thought of it that way." Jeff subtly shifts in his seat.

"Like I told you a while back, my husband, Rob, told me something we all know, lawyers are laggards. We're so damn set in our ways because 'that's the way it's always been done,' we can't get out of our own way and see the truth. In fact, all lawyers are like the CEOs of any successful company. We're like any professional athlete. That means we would benefit from many of the tools those people use, not the least of which is having a coach."

"I can tell you that because of our time together, I've certainly grown and changed in ways I never thought about," Jeff offers with gratitude.

"Yes, of course! Do you think me helping you makes you weak?" Amy asks.

"Not at all."

Amy gets on her figurative soapbox by leaning forward in her chair for emphasis. She takes a deep breath and looks directly at Jeff. "When we buy into any or all of The 5 Lies, it affects how we perform and how we show up at work and at home. It affects how we interact with clients and lead our teams. It often requires us to be inauthentic to our real selves. Sure, being a lawyer is hard, but I truly believe what ails the legal industry, what has made it a punch line as opposed to a noble profession, is our widespread adoption of The 5 Lies. If you believe you have to grind all the time to be successful, you can't possibly achieve true greatness in all areas of your life. If you believe if you're not busy, you're lazy, you'll fill your calendar just to feel good, you won't focus on doing the things only you can do, and your 168 hours in the week will be filled and, likely, overflowing. If you believe you have to be available 24/7, in addition to setting yourself up for failure, it will be impossible for you to get your priorities done or be fully present with family or friends outside of work. If you believe money will make you happy, you'll constantly be chasing that ever-moving goal and will never experience true wealth. If you believe asking for help is weakness, you'll be mediocre or even good, when you were put on the planet to be elite. The 5 Lies are what ails the legal industry." She unclenches her fists and sits back on the bench taking a sip of water.

"You sure are passionate about this!" Jeff exclaims.

"I am, because, as I've told you in the past, I believe the law is a noble profession. That belief drives my passion," Amy explains.

She glances at her watch and continues. "It's getting to be time to wrap up. Let me ask you: What is your greatest insight from our time together today?"

Jeff is thoughtful for a moment as he looks out the window at the cars passing by. He asks a bit sheepishly, "Can I pick two things? Our time together today was really mind-opening for me."

Amy looks delighted. "Of course! Let's have 'em."

"First, in many ways I'm more like a professional athlete than I understood or believed."

"All lawyers, successful entrepreneurs, and C-suite executives are," Amy responds. "If only they'd frame the view truthfully."

"Right. Second, and of equal impact, is the complete and total nonsense The 5 Lies are and how belief in them makes the practice of law harder than it already naturally is. And honestly, who needs that."

"Interesting insights!" Amy exclaims. "Now, based on those insights, what action step will you implement in order to go from knowledge to action?"

Feigning disgust, Jeff says, "Ugh, how did I know you were going to ask that? . . . I'd like my action step to be"—he pauses for a moment to reflect—"let's see, to consider assembling my own personal team, like my third baseman."

"That's exciting! Tell me more."

"We talked about how the hometown third baseman has coaches and advisers for different aspects of his life both professionally and personally. I think I'd like to begin to explore assembling something like that for myself."

"Okay, now let's get crystal clear," Amy prompts. "How will you start?"

"I'll make a list of possible candidates for the board, which will be no more than five people," Jeff suggests.

"Hmmm . . . is there a step before you even assemble the list of possible candidates for your board? Is your list the first domino in the process?"

"How do you mean?" Jeff asks.

"I'm wondering how you'll begin to pick the people to make it on the list."

"Now that you mention it, I suppose the first step in the process is to determine the mission of the board," he says. "I've got to know that before I can begin to make a list of possible candidates, don't I?"

"It is up to you, of course, but that would seem logical to me," Amy says. "My coach uses what he refers to as a Wheel of Life, which lays out eight areas of our lives, and has his clients grade themselves on a scale of one to ten."

"I'm not sure I want to grade myself," Jeff says a bit nervously.

"Kind of the same way you felt about your last action step, measuring the time you were spending on things which only you could do?" she asks.

Jeff snorts. "Yes, exactly like that!" *Except now I'm comfortable enough to actually admit it without any false bravado.*

"You can measure or not, that's totally up to you. I bring it up to give you some idea of what areas of your life could be available for the seats on your board of directors."

"No, no, I'll measure it. What's measured can be improved, right?"

"That's right!" Amy agrees.

"Also, it's better to know and look at the reality of the situation so I can pick the best people that can result in my moving forward."

"Right on."

Jeff takes out his phone and opens the Notes app. "Fire away."

"In no particular order, here are the eight areas. Personal development. Family and parenting. Career." She waits for Jeff to catch up, then continues. "Spiritual awareness. Fun and enjoyment. Personal finance. Health and aging. And finally, relationships, both intimate and social. Got them?"

"Yep." He looks up from his cell. "While I've got this out, when are we meeting again?" Jeff pulls himself up short. "Oh, sorry! I didn't mean to presume we'd meet again!" he exclaims.

"It's okay, Jeff! Of course we'll meet again. How about four weeks from today?"

"That sounds great! And for our next meeting, I'm going to have completed three action steps. First, I'll rate the areas of my

life as you described them. Second, I'll develop a mission statement for my board of directors based on where I'd like to grow
and improve. Third, I'll make a list of people to choose from to
invite onto the board."

"Wonderful, Jeff! What do you think could get in the way of
you successfully completing those action steps?"

"If I said 'work,' what would you say?"

"I'd say, yes—that's probably correct. That's one potential
external barrier to success. Are there any internal barriers?"

"Of course, me!" he admits.

"Okay. So who do you need to become so you *don't* stand in
the way of performing the action steps?"

Jeff considers the question for a moment. "I suppose I need to
become the type of person who begins to prioritize themselves
over some others?"

Amy notices the tentative note in Jeff's response. "Are you asking me or are you telling me?"

"I guess I'm asking because it sounds selfish to do that."

"Ah, I see. Putting yourself first occasionally isn't selfish, Jeff.
It's a concept we'll talk about down the road if you'll allow
it to wait."

"Of course. We'll put a pin in it for today," he agrees.

Jeff gets up from the table. He looks back and sees Amy still
sitting. "Are you coming?" he asks.

"No, today I'm going to stay and journal for a bit. I don't have
any meetings until this afternoon."

"You'll have to tell me about journaling some time. I've always
wanted to start to do that because I hear it's good for you. I've
just never found the time," he says.

"Ah, Jeff, the time is always there. It's simply a matter of prior-
itizing. Remember lie number two, if you're not busy, you're lazy?

You've got to make decisions upstream to prioritize what it is you want and think of it as making a promise to yourself."

Jeff snickers. "Of course you're right. It really is almost all about our frame of mind, isn't it?"

"You've got it. Now, off you go! I've got journaling to do." She pulls a black notebook from her bag.

"Sounds great, Amy. See you a month from today. Same bat time, same bat channel," he says.

Amy smirks. "You stole my line! See you, my friend."

Jeff turns and walks out of Better Buzz and heads back to his car. As he does so, he says out loud to the void, "It isn't about my thought process. It's all about mindset." He grins, gets to his car, and heads down the 5 to his office, feeling more empowered than he has in quite a while.

As he drives, Jeff can't help but think of the eight areas of life Amy talked about. He's also contemplating how he'd rate himself in each of them, this minute. *This is work better done when I'm not distracted by driving.* He shelves that line of thought. Instead, he focuses on the concept of awareness and how it can—strike that, *has*—begun to change his life. "Is that too big of a statement?" he says aloud. "I don't believe so." The change it's made in him when it comes to time has been drastic. He ponders how he can take that exercise further, not in writing checks anymore, but by really considering the meetings he attends. *Perhaps Pam and I can sit down when I get to the office and decide whether I can remove myself from some of them.* He knows Pam will be a good partner in this exercise because she'll act as a check on his desire to serve the firm at the expense of his own productivity. *Maybe less of me will actually result in more for the firm and myself.*

When he arrives at the office, he puts his plan into immediate action, and twenty minutes later, he and Pam are done—Jeff has freed up three hours per month by deciding he does not need to attend four standing meetings.

That weekend, Jeff drives to the beach to take Daisy for a walk. Once they finish their walk, he sits on a bluff overlooking the ocean, with Daisy laying at his feet. It's midmorning, there's a mild Santa Ana wind from the east pushing the marine layer off the coast, and there are surfers and dolphins playing in the waves below. As he feels the warm sun on his neck, Jeff pulls out his phone and opens his Notes app. He bends over and gives Daisy a scratch on the right side of her neck. "Okay girl," he says to her. "Time to evaluate my life."

He takes three deep breaths and looks at the list. "Be brutally honest here, Jeff," he mutters. "Don't go easy on yourself."

When he's done, he looks down at Daisy, who is now laying on her back with her belly in the sun. "Well, girl, awareness is important, and I've got to get many of these scores up!"

In response, she rolls on to her side, sneezes, gets up, and gives her body a good shake starting from the tip of her nose, ending at the end of her tail. "I see you agree."

Jeff stands up from the bench, stretches alongside Daisy, and heads back to the car. "Let's get home. I'm sure Mom is missing you."

THE FOLLOWING WEEK, Jeff is driving home from work, and as The Psychedelic Furs come on singing "The Ghost in You," he suddenly realizes, *Damn, I haven't thought about my personal board of directors' mission statement!* He regrets that he didn't put time on his calendar, or at least make it a task. He doesn't like forgetting things. *After dinner tonight, I'll tackle that.* He turns his attention back to the Furs.

After Jeff arrives home, he pivots to Jen, Emma, and a delicious dinner. Once they've finished, Jeff clears the table. Jen and Emma are talking about something having to do with Emma's AP Calculus course as he begins to rinse the dishes and put them in the dishwasher.

He's been enjoying more time at home listening to these two voices lately. Seeing his time through a new lens has made subtle changes in how he directs it. There's still too much to do and not enough time, but—something feels different. He knows he can thank Amy for that.

Dishes loaded, he kisses the tops of their heads and turns to his office. "What's the work?" Emma asks.

"I'm going to work on a mission statement for the personal board of directors I am going to create. To help manage all the things that are not as important as you two."

Emma looks at him with a mix of confusion and teenage "whatever-ism." *Was that approval I saw?*

Jen looks at him and smiles. "Get after it!" she says. "See you on the other side!"

"Thanks," Jeff says. He walks to his office, closes the door, and sits behind the desk. He opens his computer and creates a note titled "Board of Directors," hits return, and creates a heading. "Mission Statement."

Chapter 6

A New Definition of Success

"When it comes time to die, be not like those whose hearts are filled with the fear of death, so when their time comes, they weep and pray for a little more time to live their lives over again in a different way. Sing your death song, and die like a hero going home."

~ Attributed to both Chief Aupaumut
and Chief Tecumseh

A couple weeks later, it's a Chamber of Commerce morning in Southern California, and Encinitas is no exception.

The surf is shoulder-to-head high at Swami's and Amy is in the zone; she's experiencing a flow state where she feels as though she's one with the waves. For her, there's no better way to start the day.

As she finishes one last ride, she thinks about Jeff and the progress he's made. On the surface, he's gone from someone on a hamster wheel, to someone who is beginning to understand the difference between reacting and responding. He's transforming into someone who no longer believes in all the lies that don't serve him or his profession. He's also improving in his ownership of the results and consequences of his actions, although there's more improvement to be done to solidify his internal locus of control philosophy. *I really enjoy my time with Jeff.* She takes her last paddles into the shore and heads to the stairs. *I hope he can see how much he's changed as well.*

AFTER ENJOYING A leisurely breakfast with Jen, Jeff is out the door on time and on his way to Better Buzz. *I might even beat Amy there today.*

When he arrives, he sees Amy sitting in their usual spot.

"Dang it!" he exclaims. "I thought for sure I'd beat you here today!"

Amy guffaws. "You would have if I'd actually showered and changed! Instead, I surfed a little longer than I typically do—the waves were awesome today by the way—and threw my sweats on. I just walked in myself."

She gets up and they place their orders. Once they take a seat back at the table, Amy begins as Jeff has come to expect.

"So, Jeff, tell me about a win," she says, smiling.

"I will, but before we get to that, I want to share a conversation I had with Jen this morning. She noticed I was up and raring to go today. I let her know we had a meeting, but I didn't call it that."

Amy's curiosity is piqued. "No? What'd you call it?"

Jeff looks at her. "A coaching session."

Amy beams. "Jeff, that's the greatest compliment you could possibly have given me. I recognize how much my coach empowered me to change my life so that I could be both successful and happy. Thank you!" She reaches for a high five and he slaps her hand.

"You're welcome. Although I should be the one thanking you."

Jeff sits in silence for a moment, unsure whether he ought to ask the question on his mind. He decides to go ahead and ask. "Is that the way you think of our meetings? Are you my coach?"

Amy turns the question over in her mind. "I suppose in many ways I am, and in many ways I'm not. Does it really matter?"

"It doesn't, not at all. I'm grateful," Jeff says.

That settled, Amy gets back to business. "Okay, now on to your win."

"My win is, I didn't mark myself with eights and nines in the life categories you shared with me."

"Oh, so you marked them all tens?" she says with a hint of incredulity.

"I most certainly did not. I'm between fours and sevens in most areas with a few eights sprinkled in."

"If you're not all tens, how is that a win?" Amy wonders.

"Chalk it up to the concept of 'what you don't know, you don't know.' It's like the action step of tracking my time. I think it would be easy to sleepwalk through life and never take stock of how you're doing in a lot of ways. Knowing is like waking from that state and recognizing there is opportunity out there."

"Nice, Jeff. That's a totally different way of looking at it!"

Amy takes a beat and sits in silence.

"It is. I can't say I'd have had the awareness to look at scoring below eight out of ten as a win a few months ago," he admits.

"I bet not! It is, however, a more productive way about thinking about things, isn't it?" Amy asks.

"I sure think so."

"Amy and Jeff, your orders are up!" Molly announces.

"I'll get them," Amy says. "You sit and think about what you've learned about yourself. Be ready with your answer when I return!" Amy stands and weaves her way between the high-top tables to get to the counter. She makes her way back to the table with the drinks, an Americano for Jeff and a tea for her, and breakfast burritos for both of them.

As she sits down, before she even has a chance to ask, Jeff begins. "My learn is no matter what my score on those categories was, there would always be room to improve. For the first time in a long time, I'm looking forward to doing the work to improve myself, in all areas of my life."

"Wow! I love that!" She blows across her tea and takes a sip. "Let's talk some more about The 5 Lies and how much you buy into them or not. Are you game?" Amy asks.

"I am, but I'm not sure you're going to like all my answers," he says. He's a little concerned about challenging Amy; he sees she's investing time to help him, and he wants her to feel he's taking it all in. On the other hand, if he's not honest with her, they can't work productively together.

"Oh, Jeff, it's not about whether I like your answers or not. It's whether you like your answers that matters! So, shoot. On a scale of one to five, with five being absolutely bought into the lie being essential for success and one being the lie is total nonsense and success is not only possible without, but likely without, the lie, where are you?"

Jeff takes a deep breath. "Okay, here we go. Lie number one, you have to grind all the time to be successful, I'm a four. Lie number two, if you're not busy, you're lazy, I'm a four as well. Lie number three, you have to be available 24/7, I'm at a two." Jeff stops to allow her to digest his feedback.

"What about the other two lies?" Amy prods.

"Oh, that's easy. Lie number four, money will make you happy? I'm at a zero. Same with number five, asking for help is weakness."

"Zeros? What does that mean?" Amy asks as she picks up her burrito to take a bite.

He takes a beat before responding. "It means my wife Jen is spot on with those lies when she tells me they're, and here's a quote, 'total bullshit.'" Jeff sips his coffee and considers how solid Jen's insights are on so many things.

He stops for a moment. "Also, the work I did on my action steps related to my personal board of directors cemented my belief that asking for help isn't a weakness at all, but, actually, a sign of strength. Admitting you're not the best at something, and others are, takes conquering the ego; no easy feat. I really feel only a zero can represent how I feel about these now."

Amy puts her burrito down. "Thanks for being honest, Jeff. We'll check back in on these from time to time and gauge where your belief falls." She looks out the windows lost in thought for a moment. "It took me months to deconstruct my belief system around them. It's not like a light switch—one second you believe what you believe and the next second it's all changed." Amy takes a bite of her burrito. "Dang that's *good*." She takes a moment to savor it. "Well, at least it's not always that way. For example, you changed your views about lies four and five pretty quickly. That means to me you probably didn't believe in them all that strongly when I first identified them. Would you agree?"

Jeff tilts his head and considers her question for a moment as he chews. "I think it depends. I've known for a while money won't really make me happy. It's remembering the opportunities and experiences money can buy which can lead to happiness . . . As for asking for help, it depends on the circumstances. I'm happy to ask Jen for help, and I've also been comfortable with asking my golf coach for help. I'm good at delegating some things to staff and associates, but in the past I didn't consider that asking for help." He sips his coffee. "I then asked why I was comfortable with asking for help in those areas and not in all areas of my life including my work." He grimaces. "The answer was my ego. And letting that stop me doesn't make sense. I mean, look at what accepting your offer to meet on a regular basis has meant for my personal and professional growth. Truly. Although I didn't ask you for help, my ego certainly could have prevented me from saying yes to you."

"Those things all make total sense, Jeff. Like I said, our beliefs don't change like flipping a light switch." She sips her tea and leans back on the bench. "What would make our time together today a home run for you?" Amy asks.

"I'd love to talk about—" he stops for a moment not really believing he's admitting this to Amy. "Well, at times, I feel like an impostor."

"Oh, deep stuff today. Tell me more," Amy prompts, feeling proud that the relationship she and Jeff have created allows him to feel comfortable enough to be vulnerable.

"Everyone believes I'm a huge success and, perhaps by outward appearances, by society's measures, I am. When people look from the outside, they see my career, that I make a comfortable living, have a beautiful wife and fantastic daughter, drive a nice car, have a nice house. I mean, from all outward appearances, I've got it all."

Amy sips her tea and says nothing, allowing the silence to create the space Jeff needs.

"The thing is, I don't feel like I've got it 'all,' even after making some changes these last few months. I've got a lot and I'm thankful for it all, don't get me wrong. But I still feel like I'm falling short in many ways." Jeff waves his hands. "I've started shifting my time a little, and it's made a difference. But I still tend to put work ahead of everything else in my life." He looks down at his hands searching for words. "I'm ashamed to say, not too long ago, I felt my relationship with Jen was on shaky ground. I mean, Christ, my relationship with Emma was strained, to say the least, because I wasn't showing up for her. The last time I was out surfing was, what . . ." He searches his memory. "I don't even know when. The thing is, when I did, I berated myself for not doing it more. But obviously, the self-flagellation didn't take because I haven't been out since."

He pauses for a long while searching for more words as he gazes out the window. "The world sees one thing. Behind the curtain, the story I've created for myself is really different."

Jeff is lost in deep thought with a thousand-yard stare. He can feel the knot in his stomach growing with each moment. *Goddamn it, I've still got a lot of crap to figure out if I'm going to have the life I want.*

Amy takes a bite of her breakfast burrito and says nothing, giving Jeff time and space.

He sighs deeply and slumps against the back of his chair before continuing. "We all have shortcomings, I'm no different. I screw up my priorities, but I think I'm getting better at that. I'm not talking about being a perfect human being, but I know there's more for me out there." He stops, feeling empty. "Well?"

"Well what, Jeff?"

"Am I going batty or is there something to what I'm feeling?"

"Does it matter whether or not there's something to what you're feeling? I mean, after all, you're feeling it, right?"

"I certainly am." He really *needs* Amy's affirmation. "I guess my question is, is what I'm feeling normal or am I some sort of unicorn who's never satisfied? Do we all have different lives than the ones others see?"

"I don't think you're a unicorn, nor do I think you're abnormal in any way. You are certainly unique, though."

"So, I am different than others you've encountered?"

"A bit," she admits.

"Ugh," he says as his head hangs a bit lower.

"Jeff, it's a good thing. It doesn't mean you'll never be satisfied, far from it. It means society's definition of success isn't identical to your own definition. It also means there's a disconnect between what people on the outside see and the reality you're experiencing."

Jeff takes a deep breath and shifts in his seat. "How do I know what my definition of success is? I've always thought of society's definitions of success as my own. How do you know there's misalignment?"

"Because of the feeling you have." Amy sits forward. "It's that simple. The belief that society says you're successful, but you don't feel like it. Can I be honest with you for a second?"

"You mean you haven't been all along?" Jeff smirks. "If this hasn't been honest, I can't imagine the rude awakening I'm still in for."

"Ha! Point taken. I'll revise. Can I continue being honest with you?"

Jeff hoots. "Of course. Please do."

"By living out The 5 Lies we've talked about, you'll get to be successful by society's definition. You'll have a fancy office, will have worked your way up through the ranks, made a good living, heck, some would even say you're rich."

"They do . . . I suppose I am."

"Remember our conversation about lie number four? The one that has lawyers believing money will make you happy."

"Of course! If that were true, the richest people in the world would be the happiest. We know that's not necessarily the case," he says almost instinctively.

"Exactly. Anyway, follow those five lies and you get to society's definition of success. Behind the curtain, however, you feel anything but. There are a select few of us—"

Jeff interrupts. "You said us. You too?"

"Me too. At least in the past," Amy admits without hesitation.

"Now I don't feel so bad," he says, feeling the knot in his stomach loosening ever so slightly.

"That's a good thing," Amy offers before continuing. "As I was saying, there are a select few of us my coach calls 'accomplished seekers.'"

It's Jeff's turn to be silent and say nothing. He felt like Amy was about to share something important.

She continues. "An accomplished seeker is someone who the world sees as successful, but inside, and behind the curtain, the person knows there's something missing."

Jeff looks on, genuinely curious.

"Let's face it, by society's standards there is always someone else more successful in some way or another."

"Unless you're the richest person in the world . . ." he interjects. He immediately regrets it.

"Even then, Jeff, even then. The person with the highest net worth changes based on their stock portfolio. Some days it's this person, other days it's someone else."

"I guess you're right," he admits.

"There's a song out there with a line that goes something like, 'Even the Joneses can't keep up with the Joneses' or some such thing. Lots of lawyers wind up in that winnerless race, on that treadmill, that hamster wheel." She takes a sip of her tea.

"They're never satisfied, and they never can be, because what they chase is a mirage." She takes a bite of her burrito. "What I'm talking about is quite different. I'm talking about being drawn forward by something positive. Accomplished seekers are pulled forward by the power of their own definition of success, they use a different energy. For people like that—" Amy stops herself. "For people like *us*, the disconnect between what society says is successful and what we know is real success for us—even if we haven't defined it for ourselves—that feeling is like a pebble in our shoe. If we don't take care of it, we'll get a blister. If we're self-aware enough, we simply cannot ignore it. Is that how you feel?"

"I fear you've opened Pandora's box by directing a spotlight to these lies," Jeff says wryly. "Awareness is a positive, but it's also a can of worms!"

"Jeff, that's the whole freaking point! . . . I'm sorry about that, I don't know where that came from. It's . . . if the legal profession would jettison its almost fanatical belief in this nonsense, the profession and the world would be a much different place and, in my opinion, a better one. We need this can of worms spilling everywhere really."

She looks at him seriously. "If you're going to have extreme ownership over your life and your future, you've got to create your own definition of success. More than that, you've got to change the whole game."

Jeff raises his eyebrows. "I get a lot of what you're saying about The 5 Lies, Amy. Or I'm getting there at least. And I get that society's definition of success doesn't feel enough for you and me. But I don't see how I can change the whole game. I mean, I'm the managing partner at GH&B, I can't just change the game I'm playing. For one thing, there's too much at stake. For another, certain things are expected of me."

Amy sips her tea and doesn't say a word.

Jeff continues, his voice growing more agitated. "It would be insane to believe I could create my own game and rules to play by in my life. Crazy!"

Amy calmly takes a bite of her burrito.

"Well, aren't you going to say something?" Jeff exclaims.

Amy looks at Jeff intently. "You said there's something off, that you've been playing by society's definition of success, and you've achieved it by all outward appearances. Yet you know there's still something not quite right. Something is missing. There's more. Did I understand you?"

"Yes, of course," Jeff acknowledges. "But—"

Amy interrupts. "You've been playing a game others have created by rules others have written. Does that feel authentic to you?" She's purposefully challenging him, trying to stretch the box he's created and put himself in.

"Well, no," he says honestly. "If it did, I probably wouldn't have this feeling." He gazes out the window. "No, it's more than a feeling. I *know* there is more to my life than what society says is successful."

"You mentioned creating your own game and writing your own rules would be crazy." She snickers. "But are you familiar with the well-worn definition of insanity as doing the same thing over and over again and expecting a different result?"

"Of course. Wasn't that Einstein?"

"Not sure and it doesn't really matter. What does matter is this. If you keep playing society's game by society's rules, will that feeling you have, that knowing and disconnect, ever go away?"

"I can hope," Jeff mutters.

"Hope, my friend, is not a strategy," Amy says simply.

Jeff feels himself really struggling with the concept. "I can't go around making my own rules though."

"Why can't you?" she asks honestly.

Jeff looks at her with more than a bit of disbelief. "Because that's not what people like me do! I'm a rule follower, Amy. I'm the guy who goes to a half-empty baseball stadium and sits in his assigned seat even though there are literally tens of thousands of better seats sitting empty."

Amy grins conspiratorially. "What you're telling me is, on the one hand, you now recognize the unbearable pain The 5 Lies create within you, and yet, you're going to live your life according to the game based on those same rules? That's giving up your power and allowing miserable people to define your success."

"But—"

Amy gets more insistent. "But nothing. We've talked about extreme ownership; we've talked about internal locus of control. You're doing quite well with those concepts. The question for you is, what's different here?"

"Yes, you're right. I'm working on adopting that frame of mind," he admits.

"That's great. What better way to adopt that ideology than to create your own definition of success? What better way is there to reclaim your life?"

Jeff sips his coffee and thinks. "Okay. That seems fair. But what I'm really struggling with is, I can't create my own game."

"Can't, or won't?" she asks.

Jeff stares silently at his hands on the table. Amy's now challenging him more than he's been challenged in ages.

"I'm not saying it should be easy. The conditions are designed to keep you locked into society's game. Your obligations as a husband and father, your duties as a lawyer and managing partner. All that makes it challenging to change the game or write your own rules."

"Exactly!" He slumps back in the chair, feeling drained.

"Look, I know it's hard to get your head around. I know because, of course, I've sat where you're sitting and had many of the same thoughts as you're having," she says. "It's a heavy lift emotionally, psychologically, and mentally; there's no doubt about that. I'm also here to tell you you'll reclaim your life if you choose to do this work."

"You've mentioned reclaiming my life a few times here," Jeff says. "Are you saying I don't own my life?"

"That's exactly what I'm saying. As long as you're playing by others' rules and striving to achieve what others define as success, your life isn't your own. Not only that, you'll always feel the disconnect you're experiencing."

"What is a reclaimed life then?" Jeff asks with a bit of an edge in his voice, more of an edge than he intended.

"Everyone's definition of the particulars are different, as they should be. After all, it is *their* life."

"Amy, help me out here. I need something I can wrap my head around." He giggles uneasily. "Can you give me a hint? What was it for you?"

She is silent for a moment. "Here's the goal of a reclaimed life, as far as I'm concerned. It is a life where the person takes back their natural birthright to live a life of independence, influence, impact, and true wealth. It's a life that infuses a person's internal world with a sense of meaning, enhances their relationships and leadership, and ensures they're living the purpose they're intended to live in their fleeting time on earth."

Amy looks out the window. "It's the way we're supposed to live. To quote a Native American saying, 'Living up to our full potential where at the end we can die not with regret, but like a hero going home.'"

She stops and is quiet for a moment. "What would your life be like if you lived like that, Jeff?" She lets the question hang and is more than comfortable with the silence that follows.

Jeff, in turn, stares out the window holding his coffee cup, which is paused halfway to his lips.

Fifteen seconds go by, followed by another fifteen, and yet another. Amy continues to sit quietly. She recognizes there is a great internal dialogue going on in Jeff's mind.

Finally, Jeff puts his cup down, turns to Amy, and wipes away a tear from his right eye. "My life would be . . . whole."

Amy says nothing. They continue to sit in silence.

"Wow," Jeff says, finally. "I don't know where that came from or what that means." He's wondering where the tear came from, why he's so emotional.

"I think you do, Jeff. That is, if you allow yourself to not only think about it on an analytical plane with your lawyer brain, but in a more holistic way with your heart."

The each sip their drinks.

"I suppose," Jeff begins tentatively, "my life being 'whole' would mean I am elite in every single area you listed when we last met. I'd be all nines and tens." He pulls his phone out and checks his Notes app, "Personal development. Family and parenting. Career. Spiritual awareness. Fun and enjoyment. Personal finance. Health and aging. And relationships, both intimate and social. What'd you call it? The Wheel of Life?"

"Exactly. Now let me ask you this. What would it mean for you, your clients, your firm, your family, your community . . ." Amy takes a beat. "Hell, what would it mean for the world if you were elite in all those areas?"

Jeff takes a bite of his burrito, to give himself a moment to ponder Amy's question. "I suppose it would mean I could live a life of few, if any, regrets, and when I think about that, everyone would benefit."

"We're getting deep here, Jeff," Amy says. "Are you good with going maybe a bit deeper?"

Jeff sips his coffee. "Part of me says yes, another part says no."

"I know how you feel. That part of you that is saying to go deeper is the part that wants to know what your true boundaries are, how far you can actually push. The part that's saying no is the part of your brain that wants to keep you safe. It's risk averse, it's your lawyer brain."

Jeff nods. "The lawyer brain is strong."

"Absolutely," Amy says. "That lawyer brain keeping you safe is strong. And it's totally understandable. It's your biology super-charged with your legal training." She grins as she sips her tea. "Back when we were roaming the African savanna, if we took risks and lost, we stood a good chance of dying. The same isn't true in the vast majority of circumstances where we take risks in the modern world. The thing of it is, though, our brains haven't really evolved that much. So, we talk ourselves into playing it safe. The same brain that keeps us safe is also what keeps us playing small. The result is a laundry list of regrets when we come to the end of our days."

"Fuck it!" Jeff exclaims, surprising himself. "I'm done playing by others' rules and playing small. I really want this." He reflects on his relationships with Jen and Emma and all he's missing in the life he wants to have.

Amy looks at him, her eyes crinkling with her smile. "Let's go! Remember a while back we talked about legacy? It's the way you make people feel, the thing you can't leave someone in a will."

"Of course I do. It totally changed the way I think about the word." he said.

"Great! Now, think about your legacy and how it will be affected when you achieve your desire to be elite in all areas of the Wheel of Life. What's the one word or phrase that comes to mind?"

Jeff turns Amy's question over in his head for a few moments. Amy allows the silence and gives Jeff the space he needs to really connect with the question and formulate his answer.

"This may sound funny," he says, "but the word that comes to mind is: gracious."

"That doesn't sound funny at all, Jeff. Tell me more."

"If I'm elite, for example, in my relationships, it would mean I was fully present with those people in the moment. I wouldn't be distracted. I would simply be there, with them."

"Any other things coming up for you?"

"If I'm elite in my personal finances, my wife Jen and I could finally start our rescue."

"What's that?"

"We've talked for years about opening a place on a big piece of property to rescue elderly dogs who have been, basically, abandoned at animal shelters because of their age or infirmities. We'd rescue them so they know in their last days they are loved. Kind of like assisted living and hospice care for dogs."

Amy looks at Jeff with newfound wonder. "Wow, Jeff. That sounds awesome!"

"We love to rescue. We rescued our pup Daisy from the shelter just a bit down the road here in Encinitas."

"And if you were elite in the area of personal finances, you'd be able to build that facility and change the lives of who knows how many dogs. That's a wonderful vision," Amy says.

Jeff is lost in thought for a moment. "If I was elite in all areas of my life, it would allow me to leave a gracious legacy."

"That it would. I think it would also allow you to experience freedom."

"How do you mean?" he asks.

"If you're elite, or more likely evolving to become elite, in all areas of your life, you'll have written your own rules and will be playing your own game. True freedom."

"Hey now!" Jeff exclaims "How'd you do that?"

Amy sips her tea, puts the cup down, and asks innocently, "What are you talking about?"

"Somehow you circled back to creating my own game and playing it by the rules I write. That's astonishing."

"Jeff, I'm a trial lawyer with years of experience. Are you really surprised?" She grins knowingly.

"I suppose I shouldn't be." Jeff sniggers.

"Do you see why, in order to be elite, you need to create your own game with its own rules?"

"I'm beginning to," he admits tentatively, sipping his coffee. "I think it revolves around defining what elite in all those areas means to me. Winning in each of those areas is, it seems to me, quite personal. What is elite for me may not be elite for someone else, you know?"

"I do. I do know," Amy says.

"And by doing that, by defining my own success, that will allow me to experience the freedom I thought I'd experience as a lawyer because I'll be focused on my own goals." He looks out the window while he chews a bite of his breakfast. "If I were to do that, I'd have the freedom to choose."

"That's right," Amy says. "I'm thinking of Deepak Chopra . . . I may not get it exactly right, but you'll get the point. He talks about how the power of choice enables us to create our own reality. When you create your own game and author your own rules, you are, in fact, creating your own reality."

"I love that quote!" Jeff exclaims. He picks up his phone and opens the Notes app. "Let me make a note about it."

Amy sits quietly while Jeff finishes his note and puts the phone down. "My coach, Jessie, shared with me another something you might like. An acronym for life. Would you like to hear it?"

"Sure! You know attorneys and acronyms." He grins.

"Right? We love them. And this one is great too. Jessie told me that the word life is actually an acronym for legacy, impact, freedom, and energy. What do you think?"

"Legacy, impact, freedom, energy," Jeff contemplates. "We've talked about legacy, we've talked about the impact of me being elite in all areas of my life, we've talked about the freedom of playing my own game and defining my own rules." He considers today's conversation. "You've mentioned energy a few times today, but I'm not sure I understand what you mean."

"Well, energy in this context means the energy you'll experience by working with people you want to work with, being fully present with those around you, and operating in an authentic manner while working toward becoming elite. It may feel like happiness or fulfillment, or some such thing, but it is, in fact, energy."

Jeff takes it all in. "Okay. I think I may understand."

Amy checks her watch. "It's time to begin wrapping up for today," she says as she begins to gather her things. "What's your greatest insight from our time together today?"

"That's a tough one, Amy. Honestly, I learn so much each and every time we meet."

She pauses for effect. "Most things you already know. You're simply now in a position to actually hear them . . . so what's your biggest takeaway?"

"I think my biggest takeaway is the fact it is possible to reclaim my life. To create a game and author its rules so that I can become the human I was meant to be. It still sounds absurd in a way but also now . . ." He stops for a moment. "Obvious. Needed. The only way to really live."

"I'd say this understanding is a pretty big deal. And also, what are you going to do about it? Because knowledge without action, at some point, is worthless," she says.

"I'm going to think about the rules of the game I want to be playing," he says.

She stares at him. "Okay, good. Remember—thinking is one thing. Actually creating them is quite another."

He sits silently for a moment. "Okay, okay. I'm going to write down five key words or phrases I'll need to look to in order to reclaim my life."

"That's great, Jeff. By next meeting?"

He nods. "Absolutely." Having a deadline will add a bit of extra motivation.

Amy and Jeff get up from the table, clear their stuff away, wave to Molly, and walk out of Better Buzz. They are parked near each other today so walk in the same direction.

Jeff turns to Amy. "This is some of the hardest work I've done in a while. When we leave, I'm always left feeling both elated and exhausted."

"See you next month Jeff. Don't forget to have those five words for me!"

When Jeff arrives at the office immediately after his meeting with Amy, he opens his computer. He looks at the screen's wallpaper—a picture of Jen, Emma, and Daisy taken a few months ago. Seeing their faces reminds him of why he does just about everything he does.

The next few weeks at GH&B both fly by and drag on for Jeff. He's nearing trial week.

With each passing day, his world seems to shrink and his focus sharpens. He knows this feeling well; this trial is, of course, not his first rodeo. For some reason, though, this time also feels different and new to him. When he has occasion to pick his head up from the grind of preparing, he understands it's different this time because he's different. He's got a different way of thinking. On the occasions where he feels things beginning to spin out of control, he reminds himself he's responsible for his actions and cannot control the actions of others, including the opposing counsel in the upcoming trial. *Who is becoming a giant pain in my ass.*

Of course, trial week takes Jeff's focus to a whole other level. He's thankful his team at GH&B has his back and are handling the business of the firm. He's also thankful for Jen and Emma, and their complete acceptance of the fact when he's in trial he won't be around much. Emma, especially, seems to have stepped up to help Jen around the house and with Daisy.

The day of the verdict arrives. As he walks into the federal courthouse, he reflects on the last month. *Where would I be without all these people supporting me?* Now today it all peaks, in the most challenging spot to be in as a trial lawyer—knowing the verdict is in, and not knowing what it is yet.

It turns out to be one both he and his client are completely satisfied with, and walking back to the office, his step is a bit lighter. When he walks in, his team is waiting to celebrate. Jeff thanks each and every one of them for their work and dedication. *This feeling is why I became a trial lawyer.*

He pauses.

This is a profession worth rewriting my rules for.

Chapter 7

The Creation of Mantras

"Look for what you notice but no one else sees."

~ RICK RUBIN

It's 9 a.m. the Saturday after the verdict. Jeff sits in his home office with a legal notepad on his desk and a pen in his hand. With the trial behind him, he decided to dedicate today to his action step: adopting five words that will help him reclaim his life and create his life's own rules.

He is determined to put all his effort into this.

Jen pokes her head into the office. "Working?" she asks.

"No, not really."

"Sounds mysterious." She grins. "Do you want me to leave you alone?"

"No, as a matter of fact, I could use some help."

"Wait, you're asking for help?" Jen asks, surprised.

"I know, right? You remember that is one of The 5 Lies lawyers tell themselves—asking for help is weakness."

"Oh, I remember. I also remember thinking and telling you that was bullshit." She walks into the room and sits down next to Jeff.

"I agree with you. I've decided at least that one is utter nonsense."

"At least the one?"

"Some of them are harder to let go. I mean, I've believed in them for more than twenty-plus years now?"

"True," Amy says, as she puts her hand on his arm.

"Which leads me to the project I'm working on today. It has to do with identifying five words I can use to remind me to discard The 5 Lies, create my own rules, and reclaim my life. Our life. To have the future I want for me, us, my firm, and my career."

"I love it!" Jen says. She takes a sip of coffee. "This feels like powerful stuff, babe. These are the kind of things you and Amy are working on when you meet?"

"This kind of stuff and other things as well. I've come to think of my meetings with Amy as a chance to radically rewire my mind. It's been, well, life-changing."

She looks at a note on his screen. "What's this quote at the bottom?" She reads aloud, "'When it comes time to die, be not like those whose hearts are filled with the fear of death, so when their time comes they weep and pray for a little more time to live their lives over again in a different way. Sing your death song, and die like a hero going home.'" She looks at Jeff, and he sees tears in her eyes.

"I know, right? That quote got to me as well." He takes her hands in his. "I think the whole point of reclaiming my life is so when the end comes, whenever that may be, I have no regrets. I've realized I've been living my life like it will never end when, in fact, it can end at any moment."

Jen stops him. "But you, we, we're both relatively young and healthy! We've got plenty of time."

"I know we feel that way, but—"

"But what? We've each got a good fifty years left."

"That's the way I've been operating since, well, since I was a kid, like there's plenty of time. I know the odds are in our favor, we're healthy, we exercise, eat well, all that. We don't necessarily treat our bodies like temples, but we're not terrible either. But here's the thing, we actually don't know. Our time is really the only thing we can't make more of and also the only thing we have no idea when it will run out."

"I suppose you're right."

"I can't say I've lived my life according to that quotation, at least not up to this point. The great thing is, though, I'm determined to do so from here on out."

"Can we print that quote out and put it on the fridge? I'd like for Emma and me to be reminded of it too."

"Of course, that's a great idea. It'll help me too, in my quest to continuously work to reclaim my life. Which gets me back to my five words."

"How can I help?"

"You already have. Sharing what I've been thinking about has helped a lot. I was feeling a bit ashamed."

"Ashamed? Why?"

"A couple of reasons. First, because I haven't been living a life like that already and I know it's affected you and Goosey."

"Oh, babe . . ."

"Nope, it's the truth. The second reason is I thought you might think this stuff was a bit woo-woo for me."

"I wouldn't put it that way at all. What I do know is anything that makes you move through your life with passion and purpose is a positive thing."

"I agree! . . . So now, the question I've got to answer is what five words can I select that will help me stay on track and keep me striving to reclaim my life? Hmmm. I'm going to think for a bit."

Jen nods and picks up a book. Jeff turns inward, taking his time, thinking and occasionally jotting a note on a yellow legal pad, the kind he's been using for decades both in the courtroom and the conference room. He's at home using that pad as he is, well, tying his shoes. Twenty minutes pass, then thirty. Every once in a while he'll look at Jen and mutter. Sometimes she responds, mostly she sits and reads with Daisy at her feet.

"I think I've got the words."

Jen puts her book down and looks at him. "Want to share them?"

"Yes." He takes a breath. "Okay, here they are. Dignity. Power. Service. Potential. Autonomy."

Jen murmurs thoughtfully. "What brought you to these words, hon?"

Jeff stares out the window for a moment before answering. "It's funny," he begins. "Amy has this *thing* she believes, and it may be rubbing off on me." He pauses before continuing. "She believes the law is a noble profession. She's quite passionate about that." He looks at Jen wondering if she'll understand.

"I do believe that too, hon," Jen offers. "I think the law is a noble profession and I believe you're noble for continuing to be a lawyer." She looks delighted; Jeff feels a bit of pride.

"Anyway," he continues, "I think each of these words are at the foundation of the nobility of the law. With these words, I'll be able to"—he reflects on what he's about to say—"have my law practice reflect that nobility." He looks at Jen, a bit embarrassed by his words and the passion he shared them with.

Jen sits quietly for a while, long enough to make Jeff uncomfortable.

"Jen?"

She looks up. "Oh, I'm here. I'm just thinking about the quotation, the words you've chosen, your rekindled belief that the law is a noble profession. The words you've chosen are, well, brilliant! Can you tell me more about dignity, how that fits in?"

"When I was thinking of that word, I was thinking of my

dad," Jeff says. "You know he died when I was young, of his second heart attack, at our house."

"Of course. You were fourteen, weren't you?"

Jeff nods. "Yep. Well, my dad settled for such mediocrity in his life, both in business and in his relationships. He probably thought he had all the time in the world to get on track, either that or he didn't give a damn, which if I'm being honest, is more likely. Let's assume he ran out of time, though. I think mediocrity is directly opposed to the purposes of reclaiming my life. If I'm mediocre, it'll be impossible for me to face my death"—he looks at the quote on his computer screen—"like a hero going home."

Jen nods quietly, allowing Jeff space to continue.

"So, I suppose remembering the word dignity will allow me to remember not to settle." He flips open another page on his notepad. "I better write that down by dignity. 'There's never a good reason to settle.'"

"I love that," Jen says. "Okay, now what about power?"

"Power. This really has to do with something Amy and I have been discussing—constructing my own definition of success and authoring the rules of the game I'm playing."

"Mmm. That's great. So, what sentence goes along with the word power to help you anchor into it and reclaim your life?"

"It's weakness to allow others to define your success." Jeff looks at her, beaming. "This is great stuff, Jen. I love that you've asked me to put some meat on the bones of the words. The exercise is becoming so much more because of you." He leans over and kisses her.

"I know you, honey, it's important for the words to have some deeper connection for you."

Jeff sits back in his chair and is quiet for a few moments. "I think what I'm doing here is, I don't know, creating something like mantras."

"I didn't think of it that way, but you're right," Jen agrees.

"I like it. Words are merely words, but the power of converting those words into mantras will make all the difference . . . I think?"

"Are you trying to convince yourself?" Jen laughs.

"I suppose I am," Jeff concedes. "Reclaiming my life is, in theory, what I want to do. It could literally change my life and the lives of those around me, including you and Emma."

"Don't forget Daisy," Jen adds. "She knows when you're stressed. It affects her as well."

"And Daisy," Jeff adds. "Not to mention my my firm and clients."

"Not to mention," Jen nods.

"It feels so damn big, you know. Like too heavy of a boulder for me to succeed in lifting. I've been living a life which is anything but reclaimed for . . . all of my adult life at least. I have to wonder, is it too late for me?"

"Absolutely not," Jen says. "Now remind me what your third word is."

"Service."

"Of course!" Jen exclaims. "Isn't service one of your core values?"

"As a matter of fact, it is. My three core values are service, adventure, and success."

"Okay, what's your mantra for service?" Jen asks.

It's a minute or so before Jeff writes a few words down on the yellow legal pad and looks up. "I think it's this: Doing for others is honorable; doing for others and yourself is noble."

"Hmm. Explain?" Jen asks.

"You know, Jen, in my world, self-care is looked at as selfish. Taking time for yourself when you could be doing work, generating billable hours, and, for me, leading and managing the people at GH&B, well it seems a bit selfish."

"But . . ." Jen prompts.

"But, in order to reclaim my life and to serve others in an optimum way, I've got to take care of myself. That means serving others is only half of my core value of service. I've forgotten the other half of the equation, caring for myself physically, mentally, emotionally, and spiritually."

Gotcha," Jen says. "And I agree with you. It isn't possible for you to serve others unless you take care of yourself." She takes a beat. "Can I ask you a question?"

"Shoot."

"You said in 'your' world? Does that mean the legal world in general, or do you mean the world in your own head?"

Jeff nods. "Yeah. I think it's both because, after all, I am a product of the legal world . . . no, that's not quite right. It's not me that is a product of the legal world, but my thoughts and way of thinking about that space are certainly greatly influenced by that environment."

"That seems to me to be totally natural. I mean, let's be honest, you spend more time in that world than you do in this one." Their eyes meet. "I'm not judging," she adds, "but that's a fact. So it can't help but influence your frame of mind." Jen looks up and back at Jeff. "I wonder, is that why reclaiming your life feels so challenging for you? Because your world will push back against it?"

Jeff is silent for a moment. "That's certainly a part of it."

They each sip their coffee. Jen asks, "What's the fourth word?"

"The fourth is potential," Jeff replies. "Give me a moment here to think of a mantra to go with it."

Jeff scribbles on his pad as Jen reaches down to give Daisy a scratch behind her left ear. He looks up. "Okay, here you go. Humanity is hungry for your greatness. You know it's my belief we were all placed on the planet to do great, truly great, things, right?"

"Of course, I've heard you tell Emma that hundreds of times."

Jeff shrieks. "I've probably said it too much! Anyway, the thing about thinking you're here to do great things just for yourself is kind of egotistic, you know?"

"Seems so when you think of it that way."

"Turning the focus outward is a way to make it more meaningful. It's no longer about me and achieving something for myself but, instead, it's about others. If I achieve greatness for others, well, that feels quite different." Jeff grins. "I'm so glad you're here helping me through this work, Jen. I couldn't do it without you."

"Bullshit," Jen responds. "Of course you could have. But I love being a part of it with you." She grins. "And what's the fifth?"

"This was the one I struggled with the most. But eventually, I landed on autonomy."

"Autonomy," Jen repeats back, then falls silent.

Jeff sits straight up, and scrawls, "Ownership isn't automatic." He looks up at Jen. "You know, we hear all the time we have ownership over our lives, we have the greatest gift of all, the ability to choose. And that power to choose, that autonomy, requires us to act. It's not automatic. If we put our lives on autopilot, we may not like where we end up. That means we've got to take control. Yes, I have autonomy, but it isn't self-executing."

Jen sits and allows Jeff's words to sink in. "I never thought of autonomy that way."

"I haven't necessarily either. Now that I am, though, it creates a bit more of a sense of obligation. If 'humanity is hungry for my greatness' is outward focused, this one is certainly inward focused. It goes along nicely with something I leaned from Amy and have been working on."

"What's that?"

"The concepts of extreme ownership and locus of control. You see, there are two types of philosophies, one that believes things happen to us—that's called an external locus of control—another that believes the things that happen are a result of the actions we take. That's internal locus of control. Ownership isn't automatic is in alignment with having an internal locus of control. I own it. Period."

Jen looks delighted. "You know, Jeff, you've changed quite a bit since you've been meeting with Amy. I'd love to meet her sometime and thank her."

Jeff is surprised. "You've noticed a change in me?"

"I mean, of course. First of all you're home more. A little bit more. And you haven't missed a game that you promised to go to. And . . . I can feel it in other ways that are harder to define. You seem calmer, more intentional. I can't quite put my finger on it exactly, but you are different . . . I guess one way to put it is, you seem less likely to want to go open that taco stand in Baja. Am I wrong?"

"No, you're spot on. I didn't realize I was moving through the world differently, but I'm glad you can see it. I figured I was the only one who could notice a difference, that is, when I paid attention to what I was doing. The work Amy and I have done on owning the results of all of the decisions I make was really a game changer. It's both liberating and humbling to realize I am in control of the results everywhere in my life."

"I bet," Jen confirms. "Do you have any idea what comes next in your conversations with Amy? What you'll be working on? I mean, how does it work?"

"I don't, and that's the exciting part. After we meet, I've got specific action steps to take on a thing I've learned during our time together. I tackle those action steps. It's weird, I've always thought of accountability as being an external thing, you know, because I'm meeting with Amy and I don't want to disappoint her, I'd do the action steps, but that's not it. With the locus of control and extreme ownership cognitive framework I'm developing, I don't do the action steps because of Amy. She's not the motivating factor. Instead, I do them for me and I'm excited to share the results with her, whether those results are good or bad in my mind."

"That's a big shift for you, hon," Jen acknowledges. "I know you've been a people pleaser, which I think goes hand in hand with your service-first mentality, but it seems like pleasing Amy isn't the motivation here. It goes deeper than that."

"Bingo, Jen, you nailed it. And I think if I was doing it to meet some external expectation, the result wouldn't have been as meaningful. Do you know what I mean?"

"Of course," Jen says, smiling. "I like this new Jeff. I think you're getting closer to who you were when we first met. You're not as weighed down by the pressures you experience. You're more, I don't know, authentic."

"Huh. That's interesting." He sits quietly for a moment. "I think that's why Amy talked about reclaiming my life instead of creating a new life. It, whatever that is, has been there all along, I simply lost the plot."

"What do you mean?" Jen asks, her curiosity piqued.

"I guess I mean being in the day-to-day life of a lawyer, whether it was when I was an associate—"

"Oh, do I remember those days! What. A. Grind!" she laments.

Jeff nods. "I remember those days too and let me say . . . sorry!" They both laugh.

"Anyway, being in the day-to-day life of a lawyer as an associate, a partner, and now a managing partner, it's easy to focus on the work and lose sight of why you're doing the work. The work becomes easy, well at least easier, so stopping to think about this stuff becomes harder and harder. At some point it becomes scary.

Then you forget. You don't do it because you don't think about it at all. It's always on to the next thing."

"I think that's probably true for all of us," Jen proposes. "If we're not careful . . . if we're not intentional, it's so easy for us to fall into mindlessly moving through our lives, like sleepwalkers. Sleepwalkers following the directions on a shampoo bottle."

"Huh?" Jeff says, a bit confused.

Jen cackles. "Wash, rinse, repeat."

"Oh, yeah!" He runs his hands across his clean-shaven head. "It's been a while since I've read a shampoo bottle!"

They laugh, and Jen stands up. "Okay," she says. "We done here?"

"We are," he replies. "Thanks again!"

"Oh, don't just thank me," she says with a grin. "Pay me back by coming out to work with me in the yard. We've got things to do out there!"

She reaches for him and pulls him out of the chair. They hug, pick up their coffee cups, and begin to leave the room. Jeff looks back at Daisy. "Come on, girl, time to get outside so you can be a sun dog!" Daisy gets up and pads along with them out into the late morning sunshine.

Jeff is so thankful for his family. *I'm not alone on this journey. That really matters because this is going to be a challenge, maybe the hardest thing I've ever done.*

As Jeff works in the yard, he ponders the things he's been learning and how much he's been changing. "Hey, Jen," he says.

"Yeah?" she replies, wiping sweat from her forehead with the back of a gloved hand.

"Have you really seen a change in me since I've been meeting with Amy?"

Without missing a beat, Jen replies, "Yes, hon, yes I have." She adds, "How could the work you're doing with Amy *not* have an effect on you as a person? You're not a separate person at work and at home, after all." She grins and returns to deadheading flowers in the garden.

Jeff is surprised that he's surprised at Jen's observation. *It's so freaking obvious. Why wouldn't having extreme ownership in my relationships with Jen and Emma result in me being a better partner and father?* he wonders.

He has noticed that over the past several months whenever Emma acted like a typical teenager, he hadn't allowed it to affect him or his mood as much as it had in the past. *I guess I'm owning my 100 percent there.* He certainly feels closer to Jen than he has in a while, not because his love for her had ever diminished, but because he's more fully present when he's home. Work isn't distracting him as much as it used to.

He turns to Jen. "I love you honey."

She looks at him. "I love you too!"

"I promise to keep working hard on the things Amy and I discuss. I think I'll be a better person at the end of it."

Jen sits back on her heels, "I've got no doubt. Like I said, I see changes already." She leans in to kiss his lips. "Now, back to work!"

From the patio, they hear Emma talking to Daisy. "Those two should get a room!"

Jeff snickers and turns back to the yard.

Chapter 8

Jeff Shares His Mantras

"The big challenge is to become all that you
have the possibility of becoming."

~ JIM ROHN

I t's the fourth Monday following Jeff and Amy's last meeting,
which means it's time for another coaching session.

Amy has been thinking about today. It feels important. In her
view, the work Jeff has hopefully done around the five words
could become the foundation for reclaiming his life. When she
did this work with her coach, it allowed her to gain momentum
and, frankly, better ignore the voices, both internal and external,
which could have gotten in the way. Those voices, Amy understands, are powerful. The funny thing was, the loudest voice was
in her own head. It was always there, always trying to hold her
back from growing and charting her own path. It said things
like, "Who do you think you are, trying to break the mold?" and
"You'll fail; you're not strong enough," and "A woman can't do
what you're trying to do; men will never allow it."

That voice was persistent. The key had been recognizing it for
what it was: not her. Jessie helped her separate that voice from
her person by helping her understand the voice as a vestige of

her long-ago ancestors who were concerned mostly with survival. But their concerns were not necessarily relevant in today's world.

Amy had learned largely to let that voice go.

She smiles as she turns into Better Buzz, waves to Molly, and grabs the table at the front of the coffee shop. It's 7:22.

JEFF WAKES UP before his alarm, which was set for 0500 hours, does a quick ten-minute yoga session, and is making coffee when Jen comes down to the kitchen. "Wow, aren't you the early bird today!"

"I'm really looking forward to my meeting with Amy today. I even beat my alarm," he laughs.

"That's fantastic, babe!" She looks at what Jeff is doing. "Wait, you're going to Better Buzz, right?"

"Yep. Why do you ask?"

"Well, because you're making coffee. You've don't want too much caffeine, hon. I know you had quite a bit over the past month with your trial and all. Don't fall into a bad habit!"

"Oh, the coffee isn't for me! It's for you and Emma."

Jen beams, "Jefferson, that is thoughtful of you. Thanks! I know Emma will appreciate it as well."

"It's amazing how, when I'm feeling confident and motivated, I have the bandwidth to focus not only on myself, but on others."

"Is that really such a surprise?" Jen says as she pads, barefoot, across the cool kitchen floor tiles and hugs Jeff. "It's much easier to have bandwidth when you're not stressed out."

"True. So true." He squeezes Jen and gives her a kiss. "Okay, gotta go. Today's the day I beat Amy to Better Buzz!" He kisses Jen one more time, gives Daisy a good scratch behind her ears, grabs his bag, and heads to the garage. "I really am excited about today!"

Jeff arrives in Encinitas in plenty of time, and by some miracle, finds a parking spot right in front of the coffee shop. He checks his watch, it's 0725 hours. He grabs his bag, looks through the windows of Better Buzz, and sees Amy sitting peacefully at their table. *Damn.* Then immediately after: *You know? You're five minutes early, mi amigo. You're unharried and unhurried. Did you arrive here first? No. Is it still a win for you? Absolutely!*

His grin as he enters Better Buzz is noticeable from half a room away. Amy certainly sees it.

"Hey! Why are you so happy this morning? Good weekend or something?"

"I'm happy because, despite the fact you beat me here, again . . ." Jeff says with exaggerated feigned disappointment, "I'm early, not stressed, not hurried, and excited to share with you the work Jen and I did on my action step. Oh, and I also won a trial a few weeks ago!"

"Congratulations on the trial win!" Amy gives him a high five. "I am a bit confused on the first part of what you said, though. Let me get this straight," she says with mock surprise. "You didn't beat me here and it's still a win for you? . . . Well, Jeff, you've changed!"

As they walk up to the counter, she says, "Also, don't think I didn't hear you when you said you were excited to share the work you and Jen did . . . let's order and get started."

They walk up to the counter and say hello to Molly, who greets them warmly. "Good morning, you two! Jeff, I watched you come in. Actually, I watched you from when you got out of your car."

"Really?" Jeff asks. "Was I walking funny or something?" he says with a smirk.

"Your walking was fairly normal, but something else was quite remarkable. Now, I will tell you, I'm something of a people-watcher. I think it's from growing up in New Jersey and watching people on boardwalks down the Shore."

"I didn't know that's where you grew up!" Amy interjects. "You don't sound like you grew up in Jersey!"

"That's what people say. You should hear my brother and sister speak, they're Jersey through and through. Oh, and before you ask, exit 16W on the Turnpike and 163 on the Parkway."

"Damn, Molly," Jeff says disappointedly. "You stole my question! My wife Jen is a Jersey girl. I think she's responsible for my love of Springsteen."

"Ah, the Boss." Molly smiles. "But today it was so interesting—when you got out of your car, you had a big grin on your face. Then you looked in the window and saw Amy sitting at your table. Your grin disappeared. I'm guessing you were hoping you'd beat her here today?"

Jeff cachinnates. "You nailed it, Molly. Absolutely nailed it."

"An interesting thing happened next. The smile returned to your face, and it seemed to be, oh, I don't know, brighter? Whatever was going on in your mind, it was fun to watch."

"Well, Molly, it was fun to experience too."

They all laugh as Amy and Jeff place their orders. "I'll holler when your stuff is ready," Molly says.

As they walk back to their table, Amy asks, "What's a recent win you've had?"

Jeff considers the question for a moment, then shares that, in addition to his trial victory, he finally got a favorable decision on a motion for summary judgment in a case with some fairly difficult legal issues that he's been working quite hard on.

"That's great, Jeff. It's always nice when we lawyers get a win for our clients. It makes all of the work and sacrifice worth it."

"So true."

"That's a win on the law side. Do you have a win on the Jeff side?"

Jeff looks at Amy with a sparkle in his eyes. "This may sound a bit crazy . . ."

"Jeff, nothing is crazy here. When you prejudge what you're about to say, you diminish it. It's a habit most of us fall into and it's a killer. Now, out with it."

"So, I've got a great relationship with my wife, Jen."

Amy sits quietly and allows Jeff space to continue.

"She said something to me a few weeks ago that I believe is a win."

"Oh my goodness, out with it already!"

"She said she's noticed a change in me since we started meeting. A change for the good."

Amy looks pleased. "Tell me more."

"She let me know something she hadn't mentioned before. That she was concerned about me burning out because of all the stress I was under." For a moment Jeff is transported back to his office and the conversation with Jen—in a flash, back in that breakthrough moment in the garden. When he realized what he's doing here with Amy can't help but bleed over into his personal life.

Amy sees Jeff is distracted so, again, gives him space. When his focus returns, she replies. "It's not easy, there are so many balls to juggle and keep in the air."

"I know, right? . . . Well, she said she's not afraid of me burning out now because of the changes she's seen in me."

"That's certainly a win," Amy says. "The question I have for you, though, Jeff, is do *you* believe you've changed? It's one thing for others to see it, but it's another thing entirely to see it in yourself."

He considers how the past month felt different when he was preparing for trial. "I think—" he begins, and almost immediately stops. "Strike that. I *know* I have."

"That's great!"

Molly hollers, "Amy and Jeff, your orders are up!"

Amy rises from her seat on the bench, "I'll get our stuff. While I'm gone, think about what you've learned about yourself since we last met." She heads to the counter.

When she returns, she passes Jeff his espresso and muffin and sets her black coffee and croissant down at her seat. "So, Jeff, what'd you learn about yourself?"

"I learned if I'm not careful, it's easy to slip back into my old way of thinking. I must constantly be on guard for that."

"What's that all about?" Amy asks. "Do you have an example?"

"Ok, yeah. It was a recent trial day, and I was allowing opposing counsel to get under my skin with his antics with the Court."

Amy nods. "And?"

"Afterward," Jeff continues, "actually that evening, it occurred to me that in allowing that to happen, I wasn't having an internal locus of control but, instead, blamed someone else for how I was feeling."

"First, for goodness' sake Jeff, give yourself some grace. When you're in battle, it can be a challenge to always be on your toes when it comes to this stuff." She looks earnestly at him. "It gets easier, Jeff." Amy blows across her coffee. "It really does. It is also true falling out of an internal locus of control is easy for us to do. I still do it and probably always will. Recognizing when we do it is a good thing, though. It helps keep us mindful, and off the hamster wheel that can be a lawyer's life."

"I'm glad to hear it gets easier," Jeff says as he breaks off a piece of his muffin. "Damn, these muffins are so darn good! I'm glad we only meet here once a month!" He pauses. "I'd have to buy a whole new wardrobe otherwise!"

Amy cracks up. "I know! It takes all my willpower to not grab a coffee and muffin every day when I'm in Encinitas." She takes a bite of her croissant. "So, how'd the action step go?"

Jeff sips his espresso, puts the cup down, and begins. "It was more challenging than I thought it would be. It took a while, and Jen's help, for me to get to a place where I'm really comfortable with the words and mantras I created."

"Wait, mantras?" Amy questions.

"Oh, that's right," Jeff says, taking another bite of his muffin. "I was worried the words wouldn't be enough. I wanted to create a way to stay connected on a deeper level. After all, reclaiming my life is going to be no easy task given the years I've got under my belt doing anything but. So, I came up with mantras to go with the words, you know, to make it more real for me." He feels at total peace believing the extra work he's done will, indeed, allow him to ultimately be successful in what he has come to view as a "quest."

Amy sips her coffee and ponders what Jeff has shared. "Jeff, that's brilliant. Good on you for thinking that way. Reclaiming your life may sound simple, right? Now that you're aware of it, go and do it." She shrugs. "That's not necessarily the case because of all the outside noise you'll encounter when you define your own success and begin playing a game of your own creation."

"That's what I'm afraid of," Jeff admits.

"Before we get to your words and mantras, I also noticed you said Jen helped you. Tell me about that."

"She was a sounding board for me and my thoughts. She asked great questions. It was a nice way to connect and spend part of a Saturday morning together too."

"I love it," Amy says, breaking into a grin. "You're building a team to empower you on your journey."

"I suppose I am." Jeff returns Amy's grin. "It felt weird at first . . ."

"Why?"

"I was worried Jen would think the work I was doing would be, oh, I don't know."

"Woo-woo?" Amy finishes for him.

"Yes, that's exactly it. The thing of it is, she didn't. She was all in and said she'd do anything she could to help me."

"Jeff, how long have you been married?"

"Coming up on twenty-six years in September."

"It's no easy feat being a lawyer, a managing partner no less, and staying happily married for that long. You two *are* happily married?" Amy asks.

"Oh, absolutely! Sure we've had some rough patches, I think every marriage does," he says. "But yes, we're happy."

"Why would it surprise you Jen would help you? What story were you telling yourself?"

"What story?" Jeff asks quizzically.

"Sure. We tell ourselves stories about stuff all the time. We'll assume someone will think self-improvement is woo-woo. We'll infer from the cold, sterile words in an email that someone has a certain emotion. We'll limit the opportunities we pursue because we believe we're too old, too young, not the correct gender, not experienced enough. We have a voice in our head which often tells us something like we're not good enough, or somehow not deserving. So, what story were you telling yourself?"

"We've already touched on it, this mindset stuff being too woo-woo. I suppose I was a bit embarrassed by it. Also, I'm a freaking lawyer, a managing partner of a best-in-class law firm. I guess I felt I shouldn't need any help from Jen for something that is my responsibility."

"And . . . that brings us back to lie number five."

"It does." Jeff says. "I thought I had discarded that by now."

"Don't be too hard on yourself, Jeff," Amy offers sympathetically. "As we discussed, The 5 Lies are pernicious and seemingly omnipresent in the legal field. It'll take some time to build a stable orientation that discards those beliefs and substitutes new ones." She takes a bite of her croissant. "Speaking of which, let's hear what you adopted for your words and created for your mantras."

Jeff pulls his yellow pad out of his bag. "Old school," Amy observes. "I love that."

"Yeah, I do it for some things," Jeff says. "This is important so I wrote it long hand." Jeff thumbs through the pages to the one containing his mantras. He holds out the pad to Amy. "Here. Take a look."

Amy puts down her coffee cup, reaches out to take the pad, and digs in her Coach bag for her dark-blue framed readers. She places them on her nose. "I'd love to."

As she takes the legal pad, he's struck by the fact he feels both nervous and proud. *I'll probably look back at the work I did with Amy and Jen to create these mantras as the most important point in my legal career. More important than passing the bar, more important than making partner, and more important than becoming managing partner.* Jeff knows his confidence is beginning to build, despite his seemingly frequent slips into his old habits and patterns. *Am I perfect? Of course not. Is it right for me to want to be perfect? Of course.*

He looks at Amy as her eyes make their way down the page. *It's not about perfection, though, is it? It's about progress.*

Amy looks up at him. "Did you practice medicine at some point in your life?" she asks. "I mean, really, can *you* even read this?" She cackles.

"I know, I know. Somewhere along the way I forgot how to have clear penmanship and now my handwriting is chicken scratch," he responds with a bit of embarrassment. "Sorry."

"No worries, Jeff. I can read the worst handwriting in the world." As she keeps reading, Jeff sits quietly, hoping he got the assignment right, and that Amy will agree with what he's come up with. His self-talk is almost universally a mixture of hopeful and negative, seemingly at the same time. *I'm not sure how that's possible.*

Finally Amy puts the pad down and takes her readers off.

"Well?" Jeff asks. "Did I get it right? Do you think those words and mantras will help me reclaim my life?"

"Jeff, my friend, let me ask you this: What does it matter what I think? The thing that matters is whether having these five words and their associated mantras will help *you* stay on track to reclaim your life. That's what matters here."

Jeff grimaces. "I know you're right. It's simply my need for validation from someone further along the path than I am."

"That's totally understandable. It also reminds me of something I heard on a podcast recently. The host, I forget who it was at the moment, was interviewing Rick Rubin, the record producer. Have you heard of him?"

"Of course! He produced Run-DMC and the Beastie Boys, right?" Jeff says, unsure what this has to do with the words and mantras he's landed on.

"Yep, that's him. Anyway, I was listening to the podcast, and he said something that's stuck with me, and probably will, maybe forever. It was something like, because a thing worked for another person doesn't mean it will work for you. Of course, I already knew that. It was what followed that changed how I think about things. I know what works for someone else won't necessarily work for me. I also now understand human beings are generally lazy, and when we discover a solution to a problem, we tend to stop and not continuously work to optimize that thing." She sips her coffee. "I say this because, yes, I'm further along the path in this work than you and, yes, I did this work with my coach. That doesn't equate to me having any more knowledge about what words are best for you. I don't even know if my words are best for me. I know they work *for me*," she says. "I also know that after hearing Rick's statements, I'm constantly checking and making sure I continue to explore whether my words are optimized and continue to serve their purpose."

They sit for a moment, each lost in their own thoughts.

Jeff breaks the silence. "Dignity, power, service, potential, autonomy," he says. "Those are my words for sure. I've been mulling them over, looking at them and the mantras every day. Staying connected to them, keeping them top of mind." He believes in his gut the words and mantras he's constructed will pull him forward to the future he wants.

"Good on ya, Jeff." She takes another sip of coffee. "Like all things surrounding personal improvement and individual evolution, this is not one-and-done or set-it-and-forget-it type work. You've got to stay connected to the work on a continual basis. That's what it takes to create your own game and play it by your own rules."

"I'm coming to understand that."

"And good on ya too for going further than the action step required because you recognized what would help you the most. That's insightful."

"Thanks," he offers.

"Of course! I will say, you discovered the benefit of not merely having five words, but five mantras as well, much more quickly than I did."

"Wait, you have mantras too?" he asks with raised eyebrows, pausing his coffee cup just short of his mouth.

"I do. The thing is, I didn't initially," she admits. "At the start of this work with my coach, I told myself to just do the action step. You know, don't overthink it. So that's what I did. But I struggled sticking to doing what was necessary to reclaim my life. There was so much noise, both externally from colleagues and even friends and inside my own head, I found myself being unable or unwilling to stick to it. I loved the concept of reclaiming my life. You could say I was enthusiastic about it. I wasn't dedicated to achieving that goal, however. My coach suggested I use the words and craft a sentence about each one. A sentence which would resonate with me and keep me on track. That's how I came up with what I call my 'litany.'"

"Did that help you stay on track?" Jeff asks, hoping she confirms his instincts.

"Jeff, it made all the difference in the world. They became my touchstone." She finishes the final bite of her breakfast.

"Yeah, that's important because, as you said, this will be hard." Jeff shakes his head, thinking of the heavy lifting in his future, both near and distant. "I don't want to talk myself out of continuing to do the work of reclaiming my life, but the enormity of it feels daunting to me."

"Why?" she asks with honest curiosity.

"You yourself said things will get tough," Jeff says with a frown. "I think I knew that going in. But the more I think about doing the work from here, though, the tougher it seems. The mountain seems so damn high to climb and the finish line so far away." He sips his coffee.

"I get it, but turn that frown upside down, my friend. This is your chance, an *opportunity* for you to move forward, and no matter how far you move forward, you'll be closer to reclaiming your life than you ever would have been had you not begun the work."

"That's one way to look at it for sure," Jeff admits.

"You don't sound convinced," Amy says with a grin.

"Well, I don't really want to move forward incrementally. I suppose I'm afraid to fail," Jeff laments. "Now I see what I want things to be like, I've shared that with my family. And I don't want to disappoint myself, and I don't want to disappoint Jen and Emma. I'd hate to come up short, you know?" The knot in Jeff's stomach makes its first appearance of the day.

Amy sips her coffee and considers Jeff's words. "Jeff, we talked about legacy before. What do you believe matters more to Jen and Emma? That you ultimately reach the goal of reclaiming your life or that you continuously do the things necessary for that goal to possibly be achieved? . . . That you want to master the process?"

Jeff thinks for a beat. "The most important thing to them would be I tried my best. That I didn't stay stuck, especially now that I know what's on the other side of the door if I reclaim my life."

"What's that?" Amy asks.

Jeff looks at Amy somewhat disbelievingly. "Capital L period I period F period E period. My life the way it ought to be, not the way others think it should be."

"Now, what's more important to you, achieving the goal or doing the things within your power to achieve it?"

"Because I'm adopting a growth mindset," Jeff says, smiling, "doing the things within my power to achieve the goal."

"Right. Now tell me, has your fear subsided even a bit?"

Jeff notices the knot in his stomach has departed. "You know, it actually has," he admits.

"If you change your focus from the perceived obstacles or the seeming enormity of the endeavor and, instead, focus on your why, any fear tends to fade away. After all, you know what the word fear stands for, right?"

He looks at her curiously. "If you mean stands for as the definition, of course. If you mean something else . . ."

Amy chuckles. "Remember when we talked a bit about fear and the African savanna?"

"Sure, fight-or-flight, right?"

She looks delighted. "Yes, exactly. Well, all fear is our brain anticipating what will happen at some future point in time. Fear is short for false evidence appearing real. F period, E period, A period, R period. Honestly, it's what keeps us from doing many of the things we ought to. Fear keeps us from taking reasonable risks in our law practices and lives." She finishes her coffee. "I think Aaron Rodgers once said, 'My future is a beautiful mystery,' or some such thing. Our perspective creates this sometimes dystopian future where we fail constantly and never move forward, almost like a dark film on repeat. The thing is, that's not the reality the vast majority of us live in in the twenty-first century."

"That's true," Jeff agrees. "Any pointers on how to become fearless?"

"Fearless? Not a clue," she snorts. "I don't know I'd want to be totally fearless. Our fears can also protect us from doing stupid stuff," she says as she looks out the window. "I'm more about being brave."

"Tomayto-tomahto," Jeff says somewhat dismissively as he finishes his coffee.

Amy's head turns to Jeff quickly. "No way. There's a big difference between the two. Fearlessness means you have zero fear. Bravery means you move forward even though you have fear . . . I can't think of a time or an instant where I was truly fearless, can you?"

"I guess you're right."

"The way to become brave is to move forward, even a little bit, in the face of your fears . . . Can you recall a time you were brave?"

"Oh sure!" Jeff says. "Other than asking Jen to marry me, there's one thing that sticks out in my mind here."

"Oh, if it was scarier than asking Jen to marry you, I've got to hear it," Amy says.

"Did I ever tell you about the time I bungee jumped out of a hot-air balloon over by Black Mountain in Rancho Peñasquitos?"

"You did *what*?" Amy asks, astonished by Jeff's admission.

"Yep," he says proudly. "Of course this was before we had Emma." Jeff is quiet as he gets lost in the memory for a moment. "A group of friends and I decided it would be fun to jump out of a hot-air balloon that was tethered to the ground. When I think about it, we jumped with, honestly, little more than really thick rubber bands attached to a harness around our waists . . . oh, and in order to do this thing, you had to step out of the balloon basket and stand on this teeny-tiny platform which, if memory serves me right, was nothing more than a couple of two-by-fours."

"You know before how you questioned the difference between bravery and fearlessness? I think I'm now questioning the difference, at least in this specific instance, between bravery and, oh, I don't know, insanity!" Amy exclaims. "What made you decide to be brave in that instance, to overcome your fear?"

He considers. "I think it was several things. First, peer pressure. I didn't want to be the guy who chickened out."

Amy nods her head in understanding.

"I think the other thing was I had hyped it so much to Jen, I would have felt like a failure had I not done it."

"Anything else?"

After a few seconds, Jeff responds. "Another thing was the thought of being able to have that experience. I'd lived a relatively ordinary life to that point, you know?"

"From what I know about you Jeff, your life may not have been a thrill a minute, but you'd overcome quite a few obstacles and challenges by the time you were at that point."

"I suppose that's true," he says as he waves his left hand dismissively. "I guess I wanted to see what the experience would be like and the only way to do that was to experience it. You know that expression, 'just do it'? Well, ultimately, that's what I did." He leans in and whispers conspiratorially. "I was scared out of my gourd before falling and totally thrilled afterward."

Amy shakes her head in amazement. "Got it! If you could jump out of a hot-air balloon with bungee cords strapped to your waist, what makes you disbelieve you can reclaim your life?"

He turns serious. "I think it's a few things. First, inertia. I've been essentially brainwashed to believe in The 5 Lies because I've been in the business for so long and surrounded by people who whole-heartedly believe in them. Some of them not only believe in them, but preach them as almost a gospel."

"Yep."

"So, we've got inertia. Also, I don't have any role models for this type of thing." Jeff looks Amy in the eyes. "Except, that is, you."

"Jeff, there are more of us out there in the world than you'd believe."

Jeff is both surprised and relieved. "I had hoped so but wasn't sure."

"Don't get me wrong, there aren't nearly enough of us, but we're growing in numbers every day. At least that's what my coach tells me, and I believe him."

Jeff feels an overwhelming sense of gratitude and decides to share it. "I'm so thankful for our chance encounter all those months ago at the CLE. I'm thankful you were paying attention and noticed me. I would never have begun this journey without you," Jeff says sincerely.

"I'm not sure about that, my friend. Eventually you either would have started this work or you would have done as Jen feared and burned out. There's really no way around it." She puts her readers on one more time and reads aloud Jeff's words and mantras. "Dignity. There's never a good reason to settle. Power. It's weakness to allow others to define your success. Service. Doing for others is honorable; doing for others and yourself is noble. Potential. Humanity is hungry for your greatness. Autonomy. Ownership isn't automatic." She looks up at Jeff as she removes her readers and slides the legal pad across the table to Jeff. "These are great," she expresses admiringly. "Can I ask you a question?"

"Of course," Jeff says as he glances out the window.

"Right now, here, in this moment, which one feels the most powerful to you?"

He ponders the question. "It's got to be power," he says.

"Why?" she asks without judgment.

Jeff considers Amy's question. "It's because of the whole over-arching concept of reclaiming my life. It's so easy to allow others to define success for me. It's actually not only weakness, it's lazy."

"How so?" Amy asks as she leans forward.

"Because . . . it puts me in the passenger seat of my life."

"And?"

"And if I'm in the passenger seat, I don't have to do the work and I'm also not in charge of my destination. I may like the destination; I may not. Both are simply happenstance and luck. That's no way to live."

"You're right. It's not." Amy looks at her watch. "Our time flew by this morning." As she begins to ready herself to leave, she asks, "What's your greatest insight from our time together today?"

Jeff puts his notepad back in his bag. "I think my greatest insight is I'm in charge of my life if I choose to take the wheel. If I don't, well, I'm responsible for the outcome even though I've abdicated the role of driver."

Amy stands. "Great. What's your action step based on that insight?"

"My action step is to identify one opportunity a day to sit in the driver's seat of my life and take control of the wheel."

"Let's make that a SMART goal; specific, measurable, achievable, relevant, time-bound," Amy suggests.

"I've heard of that concept but I'm not necessarily good at implementing it."

"Jeff, just because you haven't been good at that in the past doesn't mean—"

Jeff interrupts. "I can't improve today."

Amy grins proudly. "Right."

"Okay. I will identify one instance a day where I can take a step to reclaim my life using one of the words and mantras I've discovered. I will write the opportunity and word slash mantra I used, and the result of that step. I will do that for the month between now and our next session."

"Great!" They each grab their things from the table and walk out of Better Buzz into the sun.

"Great work today, Jeff. See you in four weeks?"

"Yes, and thanks, Amy. Really, thank you," he says sincerely. "I'll get to work, and I'll see you in a month."

AFTER THEY SAY goodbye, Amy walks to her car thinking of all the progress Jeff has made. She reflects on her own journey, from a place where things once appeared impossible. From there, there was that valley when enthusiasm wavered and, ultimately, determination took over. *Guide him through that dark place and he'll become one of you.*

As she heads north on the 5, she is reminded how often she's drawn into Jeff's story and the emotions it brings up for her. She knows her journey to reclaiming her own life is far from over, so sometimes she feels like a bit of an impostor in her role as Jeff's guide. "Huh," she says aloud. "I'll need to check in with Jessie about this feeling."

TWO WEEKS LATER, Jeff sits in a meeting of the practice area leaders, the discussion revolving around allocation of support resources. Each leader wants more and believes others may deserve less, and Jeff is reminded of his work on extreme ownership—a concept none of the brilliant lawyers sitting around the table seem to have any idea about. Each one of them, in their own way, is voicing the fact that their fate is in the hands of someone or something else. *Fair enough. Not long ago, neither did I.*

As the discussion gets a bit more heated than usual, it feels like the moment to change that. "Okay, folks, okay," he says, to begin to lower the temperature in the room. "We all know each practice area has its own unique set of struggles and challenges."

The people around the table look at him.

Robert, the chair of the firm's litigation department, responds, "Jeff, with all due respect, there's no way the real estate group is suffering as much as we are. No freaking way."

Jasmine cannot allow such a statement to go unchallenged, so she jumps in. "Listen, Bob,"—she knows Robert absolutely hates being called Bob—"like Jeff said, each of our groups has its own unique set of challenges. I won't pretend to know your group's. Do not pretend to understand ours." She turns to Andrew, the head of tax, and mutters something quietly.

Jeff can see where this is going and decides to nip it in the bud. "Alright. We're all on the same team here, let's not only act like it, but believe it. We are not a series of fiefdoms. We're an integrated law firm. When one group is struggling, it's incumbent on all of us to pitch in." He considers for a moment. "The thing of it is, we're not doing that."

He lets the weight of the statement land. "I'm going to be scheduling a half-day out-of-office meeting for all of us to strategize how to move GH&B forward as the law firm I know it is. We need to not only step into our roles as practice leaders, but as the leaders of our lives. It's past time we did this work."

Andrew is the first to speak. "I think that's a great idea, Jeff. We get so bogged down in the day-to-day of our practices and our groups, it's easy to lose sight of the forest for the trees." Although the others around the table nod in agreement, none of them speak.

Jeff continues. "Pam will get with your assistants and find a date for us to be off-site. It may not be possible to find the perfect day, but we'll find a day that's good enough. This work is important." With that, Jeff signals the meeting is over by getting up from his chair. He doesn't leave the room, though. Instead, he invests a moment speaking with each practice group leader one-on-one.

Later that week, Jeff is having dinner with his family when the thought of limitless human potential comes to mind as he and Emma are talking about school. "You know, Em." He looks at her seriously. "I've begun to believe we all have limitless potential, and that humanity is hungry for us to reach that potential for our greatness."

She looks back at him just as seriously. "But, Dad, you can't dunk a basketball." She and Jen look at each other and laugh; Jeff joins them.

"That, my dear, is true," he says. "What I mean is each of us has the potential to reach oh so much further than we believe possible."

Jen looks at Emma. "What do you think, Em, do you believe your dad?"

Emma is silent for a moment. "I think I might."

Jen and Jeff look at each other before he asks Emma, "If I'm right, what are you going to do about it in your life?"

Again, Emma is quiet. After a few moments she says, "I'll have to give that some thought." She puts her fork down. "If you believe that, what are you doing about it, Jeff?"

He doesn't react when his daughter calls him by his first name. He simply says, "I'm beginning to ask myself each day if I'm living up to my potential in at least one area of my life. Whether I am or not, I make a note of it. In fact, that work is an action step I decided on with the help of my coach, Amy."

Jen beams. "Do you think it's making a difference, hon?"

"Yeah, I believe it is," he says.

As he clears the table and Jen and Emma do the dishes, he looks at the two women in the kitchen and his heart feels full.

He knows the work he's doing will pay off a thousand-fold with these two as well as at the office.

Jeff is happier, calmer, and more optimistic than he's been in years.

Chapter 9

Balance Is Bullshit

"We cannot solve our problems with the same thinking we used when we created them."

~ ALBERT EINSTEIN

It's Meeting Monday at 0725. Jeff walks into Better Buzz, shakes his head, and raises his hands in mock surrender because, as usual, Amy is sitting there patiently waiting for him. He's even five minutes early today.

Amy notices he seems to be especially at ease this morning.

"Morning!" she greets him joyfully. "You constantly seem surprised when I'm here before you. It's quite funny."

Jeff chuckles. "One of these days I'll beat you here, Amy, one of these days."

They walk to the counter and, as usual, Molly is there and greets them. "Morning you two! What'll it be today?" she asks. After they place their order and return to the table, Amy begins with her standard statement during their time together. "Tell me about a win!"

Jeff is ready for this, of course. "My win is sticking to my action step even when it didn't feel like it would matter whether I did or didn't."

"Tell me more," Amy prods.

"There came a point about two weeks in when I asked myself whether it was really necessary for me to continue with the action step every day, identifying a step I took to reclaim my life. I felt I had gotten the point of the exercise, you know?"

Amy lets him continue.

"Also, things got a bit crazy at the office. We had a couple of experienced associates give their notice, deadlines for some of my projects and cases became stacked, and I took a couple days off to visit some colleges with Emma and Jen."

"So how'd you stick with it through all that?" she asks, genuinely curious.

"That's a great question." He sits quietly for a moment or two. "It may have been a couple of things. First, I said I'd do it, and I want to be a person who keeps his word."

Amy nods. "What else?"

"When my enthusiasm about doing the action step dropped, I thought about why I had agreed to do it in the first place."

"And?" Amy encourages.

"I suppose . . . I reminded myself of the big picture point of what I was doing. The action step was designed for me to achieve the goal of reclaiming my life. Why do I want to do that? . . . Because I don't want to have regrets today, tomorrow, or on my last day on earth." He looks out the window. "Reminding myself of that when my . . . was it GAILs?"

"Yes, gremlins, assumptions, inferences, and limiting beliefs," Amy adds.

"Yes, when any one of them got in the way, I went back to why I wanted to reclaim my life for myself and my family, and that did the trick." Jeff is transported back to the conversation around the dinner table with Emma and human potential. "I even shared one of my mantras with Emma."

"Jeff, that's awesome! Congratulations."

"Thanks," he replies. "You know, I've come to realize enthusiasm only goes so far, same for willpower. They seem to run out for me."

"They run out for all of us, Jeff."

"The other thing I found was that my action step was, in fact, at least three action steps. First, I dedicated myself to the action of recognizing one instance a day where I could take a step to reclaim my life with my mantras. Second, I also promised to write down the opportunity I saw and mantra I used. Finally, I vowed to document the result of the step. Each one of those steps had the potential for a GAIL to hop in and derail me."

"What did you learn about yourself through the process you've described?"

"There may be quite a bit to unpack there," Jeff says.

Molly calls out their orders.

"You stay here and think about it," Amy says, "and I'll grab our things."

Amy goes to the counter, retrieves their orders, and heads back to the table. She sees Jeff gazing out the window as she approaches. She places Jeff's coffee and breakfast burrito in front of him and asks, "Okay, what have you got?"

"Thanks," Jeff says as he sips his coffee. "Damn, that's always so good." He takes a breath before continuing. "I learned two important things. Well, maybe not learned in the sense of I didn't know these things about myself already, but learned in the sense of bringing the knowledge to the forefront."

"I know what you mean," Amy replies. "Go on."

"I learned if I stay connected to the why"—he opens his hands wide—"the big picture, it helps me move forward in a meaningful way because I remember what the action step is really all about."

"Interesting," Amy says. "What's the second thing?"

"The second thing is new, I think. Not only does staying connected to the why of the thing help me move forward, it also, I don't know . . . I don't want to sound weird . . ."

"Jeff. I promise you won't. Go on."

"Okay. I think by staying connected to the why of the things I choose to do, the voice in my head telling me things like, 'You don't have to do that,' or 'It's okay to skip a day, it's not that big of a deal,' or 'This action step is dumb, it's not going to make a difference,' that voice quiets down. The volume isn't so loud, you know?"

"I do know; isn't it remarkable?"

"It is. I think that knowledge has the potential to be life-changing for me." He sits back in his chair and considers the words he's uttered. *What would my life be like if I could conquer my GAILs with this knowledge?*

Amy can see the wheels turning in Jeff's head and stays silent until she sees him come back to the present. "So, Jeff," Amy says as she takes another sip of coffee, "what would make our time this morning valuable for you?"

"I'd love to talk about work-life balance and how to achieve it," Jeff proposes. "I see you and think you've got it dialed in. Teach me, oh master." Jeff smirks.

"Dialed in? I'm not so sure I've got balance dialed in. Tell me more about what you're meaning," Amy says.

"Remember I told you things got a bit crazy at the office and I took some time off to visit colleges with Emma and Jen?"

"I do. Life happened."

"Yes, life happened," Jeff agrees. "I want to feel more in control and have better balance between work and home. It's important to me." He takes a bite of his burrito and awaits Amy's response.

Amy leans forward. "Well, what if I told you the whole concept of work-life balance is bullshit?"

Jeff is a bit taken aback. "How can it be? It's a multimillion, if not billion, dollar industry." His head is overrun with thoughts and almost instantly, the familiar knot in his stomach is back. He wonders, *Is she telling me for someone like me, balance isn't even possible?*

"I know, right?" Amy responds. "There are books, podcasts, courses, seminars. I've got to tell you, though, balance is indeed bullshit."

Jeff sits for a moment. "Okay, tell me why it's bullshit. Or are you telling me, for people like us, it's not possible?"

Amy sips her coffee. "First of all, there is no barrier between work and life. It's life."

"What do you mean?"

"Jeff, have you seen that science-fiction show that's streaming about employees who have no connection between their work lives and personal lives?"

"Yes, I have!" Jeff exclaims. "I think it's called *Severance*."

"That's the name of it, yes. When we try to draw an artificial distinction between our work lives and our personal lives, we're trying, to a certain extent, to be like the workers in that show." She takes a bite of her muffin.

Jeff considers for a moment. "I'm still not getting it."

"We're one person, Jeff. Sure, we have business hours. Think of a shopkeeper walking to the front of their store and turning the sign from Closed to Open."

Jeff considers for a moment. "It's beginning to make sense; that image of the shopkeeper really helped. I'm the same person at work and at home."

Now he's thinking about how the work he's doing here to

reclaim his life and be a better managing partner is bleeding over into his actions in his personal life.

"That's what I'm talking about. There's no work-life that is truly separate from our non-work-life. The distinction is artificial. It's fiction."

"I see your point," he admits. "You know, also, based on our work here and the whole concept of reclaiming my life, I'd have to say the order of the words is wrong. Whatever it is, life should always come first."

Amy looks pleased. "You've got it! Who the hell decided to put the word work first? Must have been some management type." She sips her coffee. "Those aren't the biggest problems with the concept, though."

Jeff raises an eyebrow. "No?"

"Not by a long shot. The biggest problem with the concept of life-work balance is the word balance."

"Come on now, Amy," Jeff says. "How can you have a problem with trying to achieve balance? I know you're not a workaholic. I know your family time is important to you. How in the world can you take issue with balancing work and life? Like I said, I see you doing a darn good job at it."

Amy grins widely. "When you were growing up, did you go to the playground?"

"Ummmm, of course," Jeff answers tentatively, not sure where she's going with this.

"Was there a seesaw there?"

"Yeah," he says. "We called it a teeter-totter."

"Okay," Amy says as she waves her hands, "whatever. You know what I'm talking about, that's what matters."

Jeff nods as he sips his coffee.

"Did you ever try to sit on one end and have it perfectly balanced with a friend on the other end?"

"Sure." Jeff looks out the window, transported back to his childhood. Suddenly, he's in the playground at Euclid Elementary School and his best friend, Bobby, is on the other side of the teeter-totter. He remembers the feel of the handle between his hands and his legs dangling.

"Tell me about that experience," Amy says. "What do you remember?"

"It was really difficult. No, it was really impossible. The only way to do it would be to move in or out along the board to change the physics of the thing. To balance it any other way would have required two identically weighted individuals on either end of the board sitting at exactly the same distance from the pivot point in the middle."

Amy beams. "Right! The whole concept and visual of balance is wrong. It can't really be done. Plus, it takes too damn much energy and effort to try to do it. Think of the seesaw."

"Hmm." Jeff ponders Amy's statement. "I don't think I'm understanding. If balance is too damn hard, then it's hopeless to pursue?" He's suddenly thinking of his relationship with his girls, and if balance isn't even possible. *Does that mean I've got to make a decision whether to stay in the law?*

"Don't bail on me yet, Jeff," Amy grins. "It is critical to understand the search for, and striving to achieve, balance is destined to fail. I think that's what bums people out, especially people like you and me. We don't like to fail."

Jeff sits quietly and doesn't respond. He's processing this grenade Amy has dropped in his lap and flashes back to the conversation he had with Jen months ago about chucking his legal career and moving to Baja.

Amy can see him struggling and gives him space to process before continuing. "We've talked about The 5 Lies and you've developed your mantras to combat them, to create your own game and play by your own rules." Amy sips her coffee. "The concept of balance isn't necessarily a lie, but it does cause significant angst in the legal community. Think about it, a litigator striving for life-work balance when prepping for a trial?"

"I was thinking about that very thing," Jeff interjects. "When I'm in trial mode, everyone at the office and at home knows it. I am focused, to the extent possible, on that singular task."

"I'm the same when I'm closing a big deal. It's not as intense as trial, where the timeline for highly concentrated preparation is weeks, but the final forty-eight to seventy-two hours of a multimillion- or billion-dollar deal often requires some fairly intense focus."

"I'm sure. My partners in that space lament it," Jeff says.

Amy comes back to the present. "You see, I don't lament it because I understand balance in that moment simply is not possible. I enlist my team, both at work and at home, to help me get through those times."

Jeff grins. "Asking for help isn't weakness, right? I do the same at work and at home. Team is everything."

"Right!" she exclaims. "Anyway, one of the reasons your partners may lament that intense time is because they think they're out of balance."

"Now that you mention it, yeah, it's the same for me. When I'm in trial mode, I know my life is out of balance. I guess I work to change that as much as I can."

"Yes! What is the result?" She knows what's coming.

"The result is I think I'm failing at creating balance. I feel bad about it. Then I feel I'm distracted from the work because I feel bad about it." Jeff stops. "This is eye-opening for me," he shares. "This whole concept is turning on its head."

"It was eye-opening for me as well."

"So, if balance is bullshit, what's the answer?"

"I'm so glad you asked!" Amy snickers. "The answer, my friend, is to think like a foodie."

"Wait, what?" Jeff is lost. "What in the world does being a lawyer and a good husband slash father have to do with thinking like a foodie?"

"Consider this," she continues. "Picture a warm summer day. You're sitting out on your patio because you, Jen, and Emma will be dining alfresco. The stone under your bare feet is warm from the sun. You've just finished up working in the yard and washing your hands. You don't have time to shower and change because you're on a tight schedule. Emma's going out with friends in a bit but eating together is important to you." Amy gives Jeff space to create and settle into the scene.

"I've got that image in my mind," he says, as he actually feels his feet warm up a bit.

"Great. As I said, it's a warm day. It may be the warmest day of the year in Carlsbad. Inland has topped triple digits. You know the kind of day I'm talking about?"

"Of course. It can get toasty at the house when it's like that."

"Yes. Now, Jen has been working in the kitchen for most of the afternoon. She didn't allow you to help or to see what she was making for dinner. It's a surprise."

"Got it," he says, keeping his eyes closed.

"She walks out onto the patio and, on this hottest day of the year, places in front of you a steaming bowl of chili."

Jeff's eyes fly open. "Why in the world would I eat chili on the hottest day of the year?"

"Exactly."

They sit quietly for a few moments.

Amy continues. "You wouldn't. It doesn't make any sense. It's not what you want in that moment. A foodie would want something light, crisp, refreshing."

"And . . ."

"And that's the concept I'd like you to consider when you think about the concept of not balance, but blend."

"Blend?"

"Yes, sir. Creating the ideal life blend is where it's at."

"Blend or balance. Isn't that just word play? Aren't you changing the word and hoping for a different result?" Jeff asks in rapid-fire succession.

"Jeff, didn't we do that whole 'tomayto-tomahto' thing when we talked about, what was it . . ." Amy considers for a moment. "That's right, bravery and fearlessness?"

"But this is different," Jeff counters.

"Pushback!" Amy exclaims. "I absolutely love it, Jeff. If you were to agree with everything I said without any, that would make this pretty boring. You'd be more like a sheep than a lion and I know you're no sheep."

"You really don't mind me pushing back?" He's always felt bad about doing so, especially when she was helping him so much.

"Of course not! I'm more than willing to change my views on things when I'm shown to be wrong. I'm not so set in my ways that I think it's not possible, despite what my family might tell you," she says. "Remember Rick Rubin who reminded us to allow that what works for others may not work for us." Amy takes a sip of coffee. "Jeff, it's not a 'tomayto-tomahto' situation because with the change of the word from balance to blend, the entire mental framework changes." She lets her words sit. "When that happens, the thoughts associated with the goal change, followed by the feelings and emotions, followed by the actions taken, followed, ultimately, by the results achieved."

Jeff considers Amy's words. "I'm not sure I'm buying it."

"Understood," she says as she takes a bite of her muffin. "Let me ask you this. The business and stress of the college tour, coupled with missing work, coupled with turnover at your law firm, did that leave you feeling out of balance?"

"Of course!" Jeff exclaims without missing a beat. "That's the whole point. I *was* out of balance. My life and all the things I wanted to do in those weeks were all out of whack."

"So, your thought was, it's all out of whack?"

"Yes, and, if I'm being honest, I was a bit pissed."

"Pissed? Tell me about that."

"I'm a successful lawyer. I'm the managing partner of my law firm. I've got a good-to-great marriage and relationship with my daughter, which is getting better all the time thanks to what we're doing here. Why the hell can't I balance my life?" Jeff takes a breath. "Even talking about it makes me angry. I'm at a point in my life where I should have already figured this out!" Jeff's hands have involuntarily bunched into fists on his lap; he can feel his face flushing. It seems every muscle in his body has tensed.

Amy takes a sip of her coffee and doesn't respond.

"Plus," Jeff continues. "I see you've got it figured out. The thought is, why can't I?"

She puts her coffee cup down. "All valid thoughts, Jeff. You're not alone in the world thinking those things. Again, you're no unicorn."

"I suppose that makes me feel a bit better." He takes a breath. "But only a bit." He notices his clenched fists and relaxes them.

"I get it. What if I told you all of those thoughts are the direct result of you thinking about balance as opposed to blend?"

"Hmm. How so?"

"Balance in the short term is illusory. It is *not* possible. Because you have that impossible goal in mind, there's an ever-present gap between the condition you want, in this case balance, and the condition you're experiencing, which is not balance."

"Right you are," he says.

"You even used the words your world was all out of whack," she reminds him.

"Yep, because it was true," he says.

"Yes, but only because you believed, and still believe, in the concept of balance and, worse yet, balance in the moment. Remember a few minutes ago we were talking about what it's like to be in trial or deal-closing mode?"

"Of course." He's managed to relax back to his baseline and his voice is more even.

"And remember the analogy of the steaming bowl of chili on a warm summer day?"

"Yep."

"What if you changed your goal of balance to a different goal? What if, hang with me here, you thought of days, weeks, heck, even months or quarters, as seasons?"

"I'm not sure I get it."

"Let's take trial mode. What if that was a season, and in that season you abandoned any notion of any type of balance? What would that mean for you?"

"I certainly wouldn't feel guilty because I'm neglecting other things which don't take priority at that time."

Amy nods. "What else?"

"I'd be able to focus more fully on the work I'm doing because I wouldn't be distracted by the other things."

Amy picks up her muffin and waits for Jeff to continue.

"I guess I'd also lose the thought I was failing because I wasn't balanced," he adds.

"Anything else?"

"I think that's it for now." Jeff takes a bite of his burrito.

"Okay. If you abandoned any thought of having balance when you're in trial mode, you'd feel less guilt, improve your focus, and wouldn't feel like a failure. You'd accept that life and work have a blend that varies on the season."

"Well, when you put it that way . . ." Jeff smirks. "Here's the thing though, what if I never focus on my family because I get into a rut?"

"That's a huge concern, right? I totally understand."

"It is. I see lawyers, even some of my partners and associates at GH&B, focus so much on the job, they totally forget about the other aspects of their lives." He sips his coffee. "I'm thinking of the Wheel of Life you shared with me."

Amy nods.

"If I'm complacent and focus on the professional piece of the pie, what happens to all the other areas?" He feels tension rising back in his body and fights against it. *I already* know *what happens in the other areas. I've felt that before.*

"For the period you're in trial mode or when I'm in deal mode, those other pieces of the pie don't get a lot of attention, that's true. The beautiful thing about it is, though, all seasons change."

Jeff sits quietly and doesn't respond. Amy gives him time and space to process what she's saying.

"All seasons change," he repeats quietly. "And because all seasons change," Jeff continues, "I'll be able to change my focus during the next one? I can trust that?" He asks tentatively.

Amy sips her coffee.

Jeff repeats himself, a bit more forcefully. "Yes. Because all seasons change, I'll be able to change my focus during the next season."

"You can. It sounds simple, but I know you know it's not easy," Amy cautions. "It takes intentionality and, oh, I suppose, purpose—maybe even staying connected to your why . . . it also takes the willingness to do things differently, to play your own game by your own rules. It also takes the ability to discard lies one and two."

"What do you mean?"

"There'll come a time when trial mode ends. If you're not intentional and purposeful, it *is* easy to continue on the hamster wheel and keep the focus on the profession part of the pie. If you don't do things differently and play by your own rules—if instead you believe lies one and two—you'll be eating steaming bowls of chili year-round." She pauses.

"That's exactly what I'm afraid of," Jeff says. He can feel the knot in his stomach tighten.

"Right. That's as it should be," Amy agrees. "The question becomes: How can you build intentionality into changing the blend of your life throughout the year?"

"Oh, I don't know," Jeff responds.

"You don't seem enthused, Jeff," Amy observes.

"Honestly, Amy, I'm a bit overwhelmed. There's so much change and so much to keep track of. I'd love to say I'd just do it, but that's not it. I can't be trusted." He slumps a bit in his chair and looks out the window.

Amy adds, "Yet. You can't be trusted yet. Of course not!" she exclaims. "You've had quite a bit of change thrown at you since we've started meeting." She takes a sip of her coffee. "Let's recap. We've talked about extreme ownership and internal locus of control. Then we tackled The 5 Lies. Those, in and of themselves, are big lifts! Add to those, redefining the game you're playing and the creation of your mantras." Amy grins. "You should be proud of the work you've done, Jeff. It's a big deal."

Jeff timidly acknowledges Amy's praise. "I suppose you're right."

"It's totally natural for you to be feeling a bit overwhelmed still. Remember, all of the things you've worked on continue to be works in progress. None of this is one-and-done. It's not for me either."

"Yeah, thank you for that reminder. I need to remember that," Jeff says with a little more confidence.

"You're really at the start of your journey here, Jeff. Of course you can't be trusted." Amy lets her words sink in. "Not yet. But keep at it and you'll be able to trust yourself, no doubt."

"Thanks for believing in me, Amy. You seem to have more faith in me than I do in myself." He feels the knot loosening a bit.

"Again, not surprising. I don't have your gremlins' negative self-talk."

"That's true. If you could hear it . . ."

"Jeff, I don't have to hear yours. I've got my own gremlins I am taming a bit more each and every day. Trust me."

"It really doesn't seem like you have much trouble in that department."

Amy laughs. "Think of a duck on the water. What you see is the calm of the duck above the waterline. You don't see my feet paddling like crazy below the surface to keep moving in something close to a straight line. That's the thing with the world; we're in the habit of comparing our insides to other people's outsides. It's a false picture. We're comparing apples to oranges." She stops for a moment. "Actually, that's too simple of a statement. We're actually comparing apples to, oh I don't know—" She waves her hands. "We're comparing apples to one of the letters in the Sanskrit alphabet."

"That different you think?" Jeff asks as, once again, he feels the tension leave his body. "That all lightens the load for me a bit."

"Good. Now, let's not lose our momentum. Can I offer you a visual for how to keep your life's blend in mind?" she asks.

"That would be helpful."

"I saw a video once," she begins. "It was of a psychology or philosophy professor in a 100-level college classroom. He walks in the room and pulls a mason jar out of his brown leather satchel. He tells the class the jar represents their life. He proceeds to plop about six golf balls into the jar, the final ball near the top of the jar. He asks the class if the jar is full. Of course, the students respond with a resounding yes." She takes a breath. "Those golf balls represent the things which are really important to you. Family, friends, health. Do you have a visual in your mind?"

Jeff closes his eyes, picturing the jar full of golf balls. "Yes, I sure do."

Amy continues. "Next the professor removes a cupful of gravel from his satchel and pours it into the jar as he's shaking it. Of course, the gravel, which is small, fits into the spaces between the golf balls. The gravel represents work and hobbies."

"So now the jar is full?" Jeff asks as he creates the picture in his mind.

"That's what the professor asked the students," Amy shares. "What do you think?"

"There can't be too much room left in there," Jeff responds.

"The students thought the same way you are. When they were asked if the jar was full, they said, a bit less sure of themselves this time, it was."

"The professor then pulled a cup of sand out of his satchel."

"Let me guess," Jeff interrupts. "He shakes the mason jar and the sand fills the gaps between the golf balls and the gravel."

"Right. The sand represents all the other stuff in our lives that isn't a golf ball or gravel."

"So, now the mason jar is full," Jeff says with confidence.

"You sound *very* confident, Jeff." Amy smirks. "The students were as well. When the professor asked if the jar was now full, the students cast off their doubts and, in unison, answered with a resounding yes."

"But . . ." Jeff says.

"The professor slowly and with great ceremony removed a bottle of beer from his satchel along with a bottle opener. With a flair, he removed the cap from the beer and poured it into the jar."

"Now the jar is full."

"That's right."

"But if the golf balls are the really important stuff, the gravel is work and hobbies, and the sand is everything else, what does the beer represent? There's nothing left," Jeff says, as he imagines the eight areas in the Wheel of Life.

"In the video, the professor says something like, 'The beer is a reminder there's always time to connect with a friend no matter how full your jar is.'"

"That's impactful." For the first time in a while this morning, Jeff can begin to see a way forward.

"Now, let me ask you this," Amy begins. "What would happen if the professor did the exercise in reverse order: beer, sand, gravel, followed by golf balls?"

"It wouldn't work. The beer would spill all over the place. The sand would take up the whole jar and wouldn't leave room for the gravel or the golf balls."

"That's right. Keep going."

"The sand makes it impossible for the gravel to fit in the jar." He takes a breath. "And the gravel makes it impossible for the golf balls to fit in the jar." Jeff is working his lawyer brain through the series of steps.

Amy sips her coffee.

Jeff considers the visual he has and the steps of filling the jar. "In order to be mindful and maintain an awareness of the ideal blend in my life, I've got to put the golf balls in the jar first."

Amy puts her cup down and looks at Jeff.

He repeats himself. "I've got to put the golf balls in the jar first. That means I would be guaranteeing the most important stuff is identified and space is available for it."

"I like the way you said that," Amy says. "There's a difference between space being available for something and making space for something."

"It feels like it, doesn't it?"

"How would you go about doing that?" she asks.

Jeff is in his head for a moment. "No, that can't be it," he mutters.

"Don't self-sensor, Jeff. What is it?" Amy prompts.

"I was thinking of something that seems too easy to be true."

"Jeff, you've heard of Occam's razor, right?"

"I think so. Doesn't it stand for the proposition that the simplest answer is typically the right one?"

"Bingo!" Amy exclaims. "Now, spill it. Don't overcomplicate this."

"Okay, okay!" Jeff says shyly. "I was thinking of simply getting my calendar out with Jen this week and putting the golf balls on it."

"Tell me more."

"I'd work with Jen, heck, we can also include Emma. We will get our calendars out and put the important things, the golf balls, on the calendar. We could block a week for vacation, that kind of thing."

"How will you do that, knowing how busy work is for you?"

"How?" Jeff looks out the window suddenly feeling a bit anxious. "Well, I know generally speaking what my trial schedule is over the next eighteen months. So I can simply look at that and then know I'll be in trial mode for periods of time prior to those trials. That means not only are the trial days unavailable for the golf balls, but the weeks before the trial are also not available.

After trial, I've got to get my feet back under me with the other legal work." He stops and looks at Amy, distraught.

"What's the matter?"

"It's never going to work!" Jeff says. "There aren't enough days in the year!" He slumps back in his chair, the knot in his stomach fully tightened.

"That's the thing, isn't it?" Amy offers. "168 hours in a week. That's all we get. We cannot make any more hours. A year is 365 days. Same thing, can't make any more of 'em . . . step back for a moment and think about this. Unless you actually sit down and do the work, how do you know it won't work?"

"It *feels* like it'll never work. Like there's not enough time." He stops for a moment, struck by an alarming thought. "Now that I think about it, over the next eighteen months, the sand and gravel from your example are already in the jar!" He shakes his head. "In your example, we started with an empty mason jar, a tabula rasa, a blank page. It seemed so simple. That's not the reality, though. The reality is the jar is already filled with stuff that doesn't really matter." He looks up. "So . . . what's the answer?" he asks.

"It's what you said, Jeff," she says calmly. "Get your calendar out with Jen and Emma and place the golf balls on it. Of course, the closer you get to today, or whatever day you decide to sit down with them and their calendars, the more difficult it will be to place large, time-intensive golf balls on the calendar. That doesn't mean, though, the ones you place are any less impactful, important, or meaningful."

Jeff takes a bite of his burrito as he gazes out the window. "The golf balls simply need to be custom-made. They aren't all one size." He looks at Amy. "Is that what you're saying?"

Amy sips her coffee and is quiet, letting Jeff work through the construct on his own.

Jeff continues. "Obviously there's sand and gravel in the jar already. Heck, there may even be some golf balls, and as the calendar gets closer to the present, the more packed the jar is, the more packed my life is. The further in the future I look, though, the more space there is in my life and my calendar."

"Exactly. When we adopt a new way of thinking or acting, we want to have it be perfect. We want the mason jar to be empty. But that's not realistic because, as you said, the slate isn't clean. The page isn't blank. Or is it?"

"What do you mean?" Jeff asks. "Want me to pull out my calendar and show you?"

"No, not yet. Knowing ten days in Portugal likely can't be plopped on your calendar in the next, oh, say three months."

"No matter how much Jen, Em, and I would love that," he laments.

"No matter how much you and your family would enjoy that. But it doesn't mean meaningful golf balls can't be placed on the calendar. They just have to be more bite-sized."

Jeff considers. "More like marbles than golf balls."

"More like marbles," Amy agrees. "Shoot, when I did this work, I didn't even think I could fit marbles on my calendar. I thought of them more like grains of rice."

Jeff looks at Amy. "Grains of rice? I guess I should take solace in not thinking it's that bad!"

"Easy, there, Jeff!" Amy exclaims. "You've been thinking about this with only *your* calendar!" She cackles. "Wait until you sit down with Jen and Emma. The time available for two of you, let alone all three, will limit the field you're playing on. You'll see."

"Oh, crap!" Jeff says. "I didn't even think of that! Their calendars aren't blank either."

"No, they're not. But here's the thing, if you go into the exercise knowing the end goal is to block time, really any amount of time, you'll be ahead of where you are right now. Right now, you have a calendar that hasn't been mindfully organized to include all of the most important things in your life." She pauses. "I bet you if I were to look at your calendar as it exists today, it would be filled with everyone else's priorities." She looks at him. "It would be filled with gravel and sand."

"Of course you're right, to a certain extent. That's what concerns me."

"What do you mean?"

"There are things I would consider golf balls on my calendar as well."

"Like?"

"Well, for one, the college tour we recently completed. Also, there are some of Em's games, golfing with friends, stuff like that."

"See, although there's gravel and sand in your jar, you still have room for some golf ball type stuff." Amy takes a breath. "It can be done. You can put golf balls on your calendar even in the near future. It's all how you look at it. It's your frame of mind."

"I often get hung up wanting perfection,'" Jeff admits. He thinks of last weekend when his morning was not going according to his plan for a whole host of reasons. He'd planned to finally go surfing but had ditched the plan—because of that way of thinking. That need for perfection.

"Don't we all, Jeff," Amy responds. "It's an inherent trait in many lawyers. Shoot, it's an inherent trait in many humans!" She checks her watch as she finishes her coffee. "Okay, let's wrap up. What's your greatest takeaway from today?"

Jeff considers the question. "I've got two of them. First, balance in the short term is not only a lie, it's destructive because it adds to stress and has us believe we're failing when we can't do the impossible."

"What's the second?"

"The second takeaway is that it'll never be perfect! Get started with the hand you're holding and keep working toward that ideal situation where my mason jar of life has just the right amount and blend of things. To create the life I want to have."

"And, of course," Amy adds, "not letting perfection get in the way of progress is something you can use in all areas of your life, not only your mason jar." She begins to get up from the table. "Okay, that's it for today. I'm going to hit the road and get back to the office in Los Angeles."

Jeff gets up as well. "I constantly forget you've got that drive ahead of you after our meetings." He gathers their items from the table to throw away. "Have I told you how much I appreciate you investing so much time in me?"

"You have. It's my pleasure. Shall we meet in four weeks for what will be our final regular meeting?"

"Wait, what? Did I do something wrong?" Jeff asks anxiously.

"Of course not, Jeff. We could actually be done with our work today, but I'd like to take the time to put a bow on our work together. Coaching, all coaching, has a beginning, middle, and end. The end has come for this season of our relationship. You're ready to take the tools you've created and get out there in the world and implement them. For that, you need nothing other than you and your team."

"Well, okay. If you think I'm ready," Jeff says hesitantly.

"I don't think it, my friend, I know it," she says confidently. "Can you do me a favor?"

"Of course!"

"When you get to the office this morning, check your calendar for four weeks from today and, if it's possible, block the morning out. Let's take our meeting down the street to Swami's and surf. What do you say?"

"I absolutely love it!" he exclaims. "What better way to celebrate than with a surf session." He's smiling thinking about combining the gravel of surfing with time with Amy. "Great idea! Heck, if there's anything on my calendar that morning, other than court of course, I'll have Pam move it."

"There's another thing to keep in mind when it comes to taking control over your schedule, Jeff."

"What's that?" he asks, as they walk out into the bright Encinitas morning light.

"You have more control over your calendar than you may believe. Just ask Pam."

"I suppose you're right, and I know Pam would agree with you."

After they say goodbye, Jeff gets into his car and makes his way to I-5 South. *I probably do have more control over my calendar than I think I do. But is that really true? Let's see how this works when I get to the office.*

He arrives a bit after 0900 hours and, seemingly as always, Pam is at her desk working away. "Morning, Pam!" he exclaims cheerfully.

"Good morning!" she says right back, just as enthusiastically. "You're in a good mood this Monday morning," she observes. "Oh, that's right, you met with Amy today."

"I did." He stops for a moment by Pam's desk. "Do I act differently after I meet with her?"

"Are you kidding me?" Pam laughs. "You've met with her how many times now?"

"I think today was the sixth time."

"Each time you come to the office after your meeting with her, you're energized. I'd even go so far to say you're also more focused. Heck, Jeff, it's almost like you're a different person."

"Really?"

"Yes, really. I've also seen the 'Amy effect,' meaning the energy, focus, etcetera, lasts longer after each time."

"Really?"

"Yes, really."

Jeff thinks about this. "That's really good to hear because Amy's cutting me loose. She believes I'm ready. I hope she's right . . . do you have a minute? Can we take a look at my calendar?"

After a productive half hour with Pam, where he gets his surfing session with Amy blocked out and confirms he has more control over his calendar than he realized—Pam can truly make magic happen—he returns to his work.

Over the next couple weeks, his calendar remains on his mind. One night over dinner, he asks the girls if they can all sit down, calendars in hand. Working together, they're able to discover some times in the next six months to block for the things Jeff considers good-sized golf balls. Sometimes, only marbles will fit.

When they wrap up, Emma heads to her room and it's just Jen and Jeff sitting on the couch, with Daisy at their feet. "I'm sorry, hon," Jen begins, "I know you wanted more time, but . . ."

He looks at her and takes her hand in his. "Jen, it's all good. I haven't felt this hopeful about being able to stay a lawyer and have a life than I do right now."

She looks at him. "Really? I figured you'd be disappointed."

He puffs his cheeks and exhales loudly. "You know, the old me would have been. The current me understands reclaiming my life, and making sure I do whatever is necessary to ensure I have time with you and Em, will be a process." He kisses her softly. "Yes, it's a challenge when our calendars are so full. But we'll get there."

"Yes," she agrees, with a soft smile. "We'll get there."

A FEW DAYS later, Jeff is sitting in his office. Pam has closed the door and isn't allowing anyone to see Jeff or speak with him on the phone.

There's nothing on his calendar for the next sixty minutes and, instead of diving into some legal task or another, he's just . . . thinking quietly. He feels pride that he wasn't compelled to fill up his time with an external task. He's coming to recognize the value of strategic thinking time. He knows it will pay dividends for the firm and himself.

Chapter 10

Let's Surf

"When you ride a wave, it's all reflex. It's a creative, spontaneous act. It's living about as free as you can live. It's non-think. In that moment you are in sync with the heartbeat of the earth."

~ MICKEY MUÑOZ

The day of their final session, the San Diego morning dawns clear and warm. A mild Santa Ana wind is blowing from the east and the sky is an unbelievably deep blue. The surf is, well perhaps perfect is too strong of a word, but, perhaps not at all.

Amy is standing in the parking lot at the top of Swami's, a Yeti travel mug of coffee in her hands. She is reflecting on her time meeting with Jeff and how she hopes he's now well on the road to reclaiming his life, serving his clients from a more authentic place, guiding his law firm as only he can, and being the husband, father, friend, and community member he can be. Something that only comes once lawyers like him—and, if she's being totally honest, her—do the hard work of getting off the damn hamster wheel and living an intentional life infused with purpose. As she gazes out at this morning's chest-to-head-high sets at Swami's, she is smiling.

JEFF DRIVES DOWN the 101 through Encinitas, the radio play-ing softly in the background. He too has a Yeti travel mug of cof-fee resting in the center console. He is—if he's being honest with himself—a bit nervous about today. It's not the surf that has him concerned, or surfing with Amy for the first time. Over these past six months, he's gotten to know her fairly well, although as he reflects on their time together, he realizes he's done most of the talking. No, this morning Jeff fears whether he'll be able to maintain his focus, momentum, and enthusiasm to reclaim his life when he's no longer meeting with her.

She's been a great accountability and motivational presence in his life. He recognizes the work he's doing to reclaim his life amounts to a battle not only for his future, but for the future of his family. But that's not all. It's also a fight for the future of so many others, from his family to the law firm to his community. As he drives down the coast highway, he mutters, *Can I do this without the steadying influence and wisdom of Amy?*

He turns into the parking lot, chortles when he sees her. *Of course she's here already.* By now, he wouldn't have it any other way.

Jeff parks next to Amy and pops his trunk. "Hi, Coach! How's the surf looking?"

"Pretty good this morning, Grasshopper." She grins.

"Grasshopper!" He shakes his head. "Love the Kung Fu refer-ence." He bows. "Master Po."

They both laugh as Amy puts her coffee mug on the roof of her car and opens the trunk. They both get into their spring wetsuits as the water temperature has warmed up quite nicely, at least for a couple of surfers accustomed to the San Diego coastal waters. As they chitchat, Amy notices Jeff appears to be a bit distracted.

"What's up, Jeff?" she asks. "You seem a bit, oh I don't know, off?"

Jeff looks past Amy out at the Pacific and the horizon. "It's not the same meeting with you without seeing Molly!" Even his attempt at humor falls a bit flat.

Amy looks at him squarely in the eye as she grabs the pull on her wetsuit and zips herself up. "I know, right?" she says, knowing full well that's not it. That's not what's going on.

Jeff grabs his small pack with surf wax. "Amy, I've got wax," he says, and they each grab their boards.

"This never gets old, does it?" he says as Amy grabs her coffee, and they make their way down the 145 stairs to the beach.

She looks back over her left shoulder. "When it does, that'll be the end of me." They both laugh.

When they get to the sand, they put their boards down and Jeff unsolders his bag, removes his surf wax, breaks a hunk off for Amy, and tosses it to her. They both drop to their knees and go about waxing their boards in relative silence. Jeff is concentrating on waxing his board. As he does so he cannot help but notice the feel of the cool sand between his toes.

"Hey, Jeff?"

"Hmm?" he says, lost in thought.

"Seriously, what's up? I mean I like seeing Molly as much as anyone, but that's not what's got you this morning. I know you a bit better than that."

Jeff stops waxing his surfboard, looks up, and gives a half-hearted grin. "Yes, you do," he says. "I'm just feeling nervous."

She sits down on the sand next to her board. "About surfing with me?" She snorts. "Come on now . . ."

"Of course not! It's not that at all!" He smiles, feeling a bit defensive at the same time.

"Okay, so what gives? You know your head needs to be right to get the most out of your surf session. If you go into it with negative thoughts, it won't be the same."

"Awfully Zen of you, Amy. Of course you're right . . . I'm worried we won't be meeting anymore."

"Tell me more," she prompts.

"Well," he begins, "I'm afraid I'll lose momentum on reclaiming my life." He gazes out over the ocean. "You know, I didn't have any type of handle on it when we met, and I was headed to burnout and worse. The thought of losing momentum and returning to my old ways scares the hell out of me."

She's quiet for a few beats. "Listen, Jeff," Amy says, "I totally get it. When Jessie first suggested we take a break from our coaching relationship so that I could try out the new tools I'd learned, I was, frankly, freaked-the-hell out. I'm not in your exact shoes, but I've been in the position you're in today. I get it."

"Did you lose momentum?" Jeff asks.

"Honestly, yes, I did," Amy says as she begins to stand up. She wipes the sand from her bottom, then from her hands. "Let's paddle out and we can chat out there." She points to the ocean. "And remember, the ocean can feel your vibes!" She grabs her board and begins to walk toward the surf. Jeff stands, brushes the sand off his hands, grabs his board, and follows.

"How'd you deal with it? With losing momentum?" he asks as he catches up to her.

"This may sound simple," she begins. "I simply decided the fear and pain of *not* moving forward was greater than the fear and pain of doing so. In other words," she says as her feet hit the water, "I decided to use my natural tendency of being gritty to decide to move forward."

Jeff's feet hit the water. Even though it's spring-suit temperature, it's still refreshing on his toes.

Amy turns to him. "Come on, let's get out there!" She begins to execute a perfect stingray shuffle until she's up to her hips in the cool clear Pacific, throws her board down, flops on it and begins to paddle. Jeff executes the same maneuvers and follows her.

The two lawyers paddle out through the white water and the shore break under an impossibly clear cobalt-blue sky. They paddle in silence to their chosen spot to post up, beyond the point break that is Swami's. They each pop up and sit on their board. Both are smiling.

Jeff looks at the Pacific all around them. "Ah!" he proclaims. "This is what it's all about."

"Indeed it is, Jeff." Amy grins as she slicks her salt-and-pepper hair back from her face. "Indeed it is. Now, we're out here in this awesome and breathtaking environment. Let's surf and talk." She continues. "We kind of got off track this morning."

"What do you mean?"

"I didn't ask you about your win! Let's change the frame and mentally step away from your fear, which I promise we'll talk about, and get you set up for success. Tell me about a win."

Jeff considers her question for a moment. "I've got several. Jen, Emma, and I coordinated our calendars so we could place golf balls and marbles on them to stay connected. The main one, though, is being out here this morning with you."

"Tell me more," she prods, as she looks oceanward for a wave to catch.

"Immediately after our last meeting, I went to the office and coordinated with Pam to arrange my schedule to allow this to happen."

"Two questions," Amy says. "First, what was Pam's reaction, and second, how'd it feel?"

"Pam was all on board. She was more than happy to help me block this time by rescheduling a couple of appointments I had. As far as how it felt," he says, as he looks out at a perfect set of three waves approaching,[8] "it was amazing. It allowed me to experience a sense of control I forgot I had. I felt that same sense of control when the family got their calendars together."

Amy spies the set as well. She lays down on her board and begins to paddle, pointing the nose of her board expertly in the perfect direction. "I'm taking this one, you get the third wave in the set." She executes a perfect paddle and pop up and surfs down the face of a shoulder-high right-hand breaking wave.

Jeff lets the wave go and catches the last wave in the set. He too executes a perfect paddle and pop up, riding the face of the wave to his right and traveling between the trough and crest. He shallow-dives off near Amy and they both begin to paddle out.

"Great ride!" Amy exclaims. "You're a pretty good surfer," she jokes.

"You too!" Jeff responds, laughing.

When they get back out past the break, they smoothly post up again waiting for the next set.

Amy asks, "What did you learn about yourself in making sure this meeting happened?"

"I suppose I learned a few things. First, I have more control over my schedule than I remembered. I was also reminded Pam is a great teammate and an invaluable resource when it comes to my schedule and what gets placed on it."

"Our assistants, to the extent we actually allow them to do their jobs, are fantastic resources and guardians when it comes to our calendars. The key, of course, is letting them do their jobs!"

"So true," he admits as he splashes cool ocean water on his face. They each gaze west in search of the next set of waves. There are none on the horizon.

---

8 What most non-surfers don't know is that surfing can be as much as 90 percent waiting for a wave and 10 percent surfing. There's plenty of time for conversation; when done properly, surfing is also a social event.

Jeff says, "Let's get back to momentum."

"Of course. When it comes to momentum in reclaiming your life and, in fact, in any aspect of our lives, it's all about never stopping. What we're doing here is a perfect visual. When you paddle to catch a wave, what happens if you stop?"

"The wave passes me by. I can't catch it," Jeff offers.

"Precisely. If you don't stop, as you paddle, you'll get to the point where you'll give two final powerful digs and pop up. Your momentum and the wave do the rest."

"Sure," Jeff agrees. "But how do I translate that into my desire . . . no that's not the right word . . . my yearning to reclaim my life?" he asks, as he swirls his legs to maintain his position.

"I'm not sure, Jeff," Amy says. "Now that you have the visual, how *do* you do it?" She lies down on her board. "Think about that question while I catch this wave." She smoothly turns the nose of her board shoreward and begins to paddle.

"Oh no you don't." He turns his board as well. "We can both ride this one."

They both paddle but don't catch the wave; it passes beneath them cresting a few feet shoreward. "The beautiful thing about this," Jeff says as he turns his board to paddle out a bit, "is there's always another wave."

Amy turns her board and catches up to Jeff. "That's right. There's always another wave and there's always another opportunity to reclaim your life."

Jeff paddles next to Amy. "How do you do it?"

"Not so fast, my friend." She laughs. "Remember what Rick Rubin says—because it worked for me doesn't necessarily mean it'll work for you. Also, because it's the way I'm doing it, doesn't mean it's the best way to get it done. I'm as lazy as the next person, so when I land on something that works, I will use it and often stop looking for a better way."

They reach their spot in the ocean and both sit up and straddle their boards, gazing at the horizon.

"So, the question is, Jeff, how will *you* do it?"

Jeff ponders the question as he gently moves his hands through the water. "Maybe it's as simple as continuing to do all the stuff we've worked on."

"Get more detailed," Amy encourages.

"Well, I suppose the first thing is to keep my internal locus of control. I need to own my life and all the results. It truly is all up to me. If I make decisions and choices that move me closer to the goal of reclaiming my life, it will eventually happen. If I don't, it most assuredly won't."

"How will you continue to build that muscle, the one where you factor into each decision and choice whether it moves you forward?" Amy asks.

"That's just it, isn't it?" Jeff says. "It's building that muscle a little bit every day so it almost becomes automatic." He considers what to say next. "I'll create space to consider not only the immediate results which, if we're being honest, will most likely appear to either have no effect on my reclamation project or, on the surface, appear to further the goal. I will ask myself before making a decision or a choice what the second and third-level consequences of the choice will be."

"What's one concrete step you can take in implementing that system?" Amy asks as she spies a nice set approaching.

"I'll begin with a goal of using that system once a day and build from there. I'll track that goal in my planner," he says. He too sees the approaching set, turns his board, and lies prone paddling gently as the first wave approaches.

"Sounds like a plan," Amy says as she also sets herself up for the set. "I'm waiting for the next one."

Jeff likes the shape of the first wave in the set and so begins to paddle. At the exact right moment, he digs powerfully, twice, feeling the weight of the ocean against his hands, which he plants under his lower ribs. He pushes the top of his body up off the board, turns his hips to the right, and moves his left leg to the front of the board, landing perfectly in a squat with his feet in the ideal position. Then he slides down the face of the wave. He is focused solely on riding the wave; any other thoughts fade away to nothingness.

True to her word, Amy catches the second wave. She drops in a bit late, but is able to use the power of the wave and her momentum to catch up and has a great ride. She gracefully falls off in Jeff's vicinity.

"Nice save, Amy," Jeff says. "It looked like you were a bit late to the party there."

"I was, indeed," she agrees. "It's amazing what happens when you let the ride just unfold and become one with the wave. That one certainly stretched the challenge-skill ratio, and it helped me find flow."

"Flow?" Jeff asks.

"You know, when you're in the zone." They begin to paddle back out. "It's flow and it's all based on biology and neurochemistry."

"Ah, gotcha. I love that sensation," Jeff says.

"Me too. The beautiful thing is you can create that, essentially on demand, if you know what you're doing. Heck, you can even create it at work."

"How'd you learn about that?" Jeff asks, as they reach their spot to wait for the next set.

"My coach, of course," Amy says. "Let's not lose the thread here, Jeff. We're focused on how you'll be able to maintain your momentum and reclaim your life?"

"I need to become comfortable with being uncomfortable," he says as he paddles out.

"I'm not sure I get it," Amy says.

"Well, I'm comfortable playing the game others have created for me. So comfortable, it seems, I've become numb to the consequences playing that game has to my life and the lives of those I love." He shakes his head. "I need to get comfortable with being uncomfortable because if I'm playing my own game by my own rules, some feathers are bound to be ruffled."

"Whose feathers are you most concerned about ruffling?"

"Probably my law partners." Jeff stops paddling and sits up and straddles his board.

"How will you lead through that transition period from playing the game others have created to playing your game by your rules and achieving your own vision of success?" Amy says.

A wave passes beneath them as Jeff considers the question.

"I never thought about having to lead others through the transition. That adds another layer to the fear."

"Remember, Jeff, fear stands for false evidence appearing real. It's nothing but the story you're telling yourself."

"I suppose I'll lead as you've led me through the beginning of the process. After I decide on my game and define my rules, I'll sit with them individually and let them know what's going on and why things are going to be different."

"How will you answer the question every one of them is sure to have: How will this affect the firm's bottom line?"

"I'll show them proof it'll improve it. We have been meeting for six months, and I've been working my mantras for the past four of them?"

"Sounds about right."

"During that time, I've been more productive, more focused, and, frankly, happier. If I can do it, what would it mean for the firm if we all did the work of reclaiming our lives?"

"What would it mean indeed?" Amy posits, as she turns her

board and begins paddling. "You've also got to consider the power dynamics at play with your game plan."

Jeff allows the wave to pass. He's pondering Amy's question and warning. He comes out of his revery as a beautiful wave begins to form on the horizon. As he paddles into the wave, he reflects, *What kind of law firm would we have if that happened?* He pops up on the wave and drops right back into the zone of being one with the sea.

Amy paddles out and passes behind him on the wave, duck-diving her board through the breaking surf.

Jeff finishes his ride and paddles back to Amy.

"Jeff, you looked awesome on that wave, so relaxed. Tell me, what was going through your mind?"

"Honestly, when I was riding the wave, absolutely nothing was going through my mind. It was totally blank. I was just feeling the wave. Now, what I was thinking before I dropped in? That's something totally different."

Amy raises her eyebrows.

"I was wondering what kind of law firm we'd have if all of us, beginning of course with the partners, set about reclaiming our lives," Jeff says.

"What do you think?" Amy asks.

"I think if we're world-class now, we'd be so much better afterward. So damn much better. I also know, as you correctly pointed out, that power dynamics preclude me from being the coach. So, what do you say, Amy, will you come and coach all of us?"

"Oh, Jeff, that's nice of you to ask. And my answer is absolutely not! I'm not a coach, I don't have any formal training. What we've been doing is merely scratching the surface of what a coach can do with you. Plus, you're a bunch of high-achieving lawyers, I'm like your lot. No, what your law firm needs is a Certified Professional Coach who focuses on coaching lawyers."

"Do you know anyone like that?" Jeff says with a grin.

"As a matter of fact, I do! I think you're now ready to meet him." She looks at Jeff knowingly. "But, let's not get off track. We've been talking about how you'll maintain your momentum in reclaiming *your* life. Let's not let the worry about your partners derail us from our conversation."

"Okay, okay!" Jeff relents. "I'm thrilled with the possibility of creating the law firm I see is possible."

"So far you talked about creating a system where you challenge yourself to think of secondary and tertiary consequences to the decisions you make and whether the decision, ultimately, leads you on the path to reclaiming your life. That's the internal locus of control part. Next, you mentioned creating your own game and your own rules. What'd you call that?" she asks.

"I need to get comfortable with being uncomfortable," he says.

"Right. In that space you talked about creating a team and a culture at your firm that would encourage everyone to do the same."

"Yep. I think that's a fantastic way of decreasing the discomfort," he says. "If we're all doing it, it would feel less uncomfortable."

"What will you do if you encounter resistance? Surely you can think of a partner who won't initially follow your lead."

"Oh, I can indeed. I've got two of 'em."

"Actually, I know I asked, but let's not bring your GAILs here!" she sniggers. "That's nothing more than an assumption. You never know until you try."

"True. Let's presume for the sake of this discussion, though, I'm right. The question is, how do I keep my own momentum in the face of that?" Jeff asks.

"Yes. How do you not let the bastards get you down?"

"Ha! I think that's where the remainder of the team, including Jen and Emma, come in. I've got to remember, no matter what,

I'm not on this journey alone. I've got a supportive team wanting me to succeed."

"Anything else?" Amy asks.

"I think this is where staying connected to the mantras comes in."

"Tell me about that."

Just then, another surfer joins their pod. "Hey Amy! How's it going?"

"Hey!" she exclaims. "What are you doing here? It's great to see you!"

The stranger begins to turn his board shoreward. Amy and Jeff gaze out and see what appears to be the best set of the day approaching them. They turn their boards as well.

Jeff says, "Nice set of three," and begins to paddle.

Amy and the stranger let him take the first wave; they each take the others.

When they've each finished their rides, they turn and paddle out together.

"So, Amy," Jeff begins as he smiles at the stranger, "who's your friend?"

"Oh," Amy says a bit embarrassed. "I was so focused on our conversation and so surprised when this guy showed up, I totally forgot. You two don't know each other!"

"Jeff," Amy says, "this is Jessie. Jessie, this is Jeff."

"Hold on." Jeff stops. "Amy, is this *the* Jessie? Your coach?"

Amy and Jessie glance at each other conspiratorially.

"Yes, Jeff," Amy confesses, "this is my coach, Jessie. Who you've heard so much about." She grins.

"Well Jeff, knowing that, I hope we can still be friends!" Jessie laughs.

"I hope so too," Jeff answers enthusiastically. "And I should ask you the same question! What has Amy told you about me?"

"Nothing in particular. Honestly," Jessie says. "She just let me know she was exploring in my sandbox and asked if it was okay."

"I did, indeed." Amy says. "Although I wouldn't say I was in your entire sandbox, Jessie. I was at the edges. There's no way I could do what you do."

"That may be true, Amy. It's not for lack of talent, though. It's simply because we're all unique. You've got your own gifts."

"Back to your question, though, Jeff." Jessie turns to him. "Amy has not told me one thing about you and the work you've been doing. What goes on between a coach and their client is confidential. That's the only way it works."

"The funny thing," Jeff begins, "is I *really* believe you."

Amy feigns shock. "The *funny* thing?"

"That's not what I meant," Jeff interjects, embarrassed.

There's a moment of quiet among the three surfers; the only sounds to be heard are the crashing waves and a lone seagull.

"So, Jeff," Jessie says, "tell me about your mantras. What's the deal with them?"

"I'm a lawyer, you know that much about me, right?" Jeff asks. Jessie nods his head. "I came up with five mantras to help me remember to reclaim my life."

"I love it!" Jessie says approvingly. "Tell me more."

"So that's where Amy gets it!" Jeff exclaims.

Amy and Jessie look at each other in confusion.

"'Tell me more,'" Jeff clarifies. The three of them burst out laughing because they've all heard that statement before.

Jessie looks at the incoming set. "It's one of the best questions any coach can ask! But, for now, hold that thought; here comes my wave." Jessie turns and sets up for the wave, pops up, and speeds down the face.

"And this one, Amy, is mine!" Jeff exclaims as he spins, paddles, and pops up."

"Hey, what ever happened to ladies first, you two?" Amy says with a laugh, more to herself than anyone else. After she catches the third wave of the set, the three surfers meet up and paddle out through the breaking waves, duck-diving, turtle-rolling, and gliding over the peaking waves before they crest. As they do so, their conversation picks back up.

"So, Jeff," Jessie begins. "Tell me about your mantras."

Jeff spits out a stream of salty ocean water. "I believe every human being has the ability to embody these five things: dignity, power, service, potential, and autonomy. The thing about them, though, is you've got to put in the work to live those principles."

"I love those words," Jessie compliments, "and I couldn't agree more with your statement about putting in the work."

"That's the reason for the five mantras, to remind me to put in the work. For dignity, my mantra is there's never a good reason to settle. For power, my mantra is, it's weakness to allow others to define your success."

"I really like that one, Jeff," Amy offers. "If you were to ask me, that's the key to continuing to do the work of reclaiming your life, creating your own game, and authoring your own rules."

"Bingo!" Jeff exclaims. "I've been worried about how I would stay focused and maintain my momentum because my meetings with Amy are coming to an end, Jessie. You're right, though, if I really lean into my power mantra, I can't help but maintain my focus."

"Right," Jessie says. "What are your others?"

"Sorry, this one may sound a bit on the corny side, but it's mine and I love it. For service, my mantra is, doing for others is honorable; doing for others and yourself is noble."

"Jeff, if you're playing your own game by your own rules, you've got to ditch apologizing for something that resonates with you. You have nothing to apologize for, so cut it out," Jessie says seriously. "Besides, I think you nailed it. Lawyers think self-care is selfish. They forget they are the most important part of their law practice and if they don't take care of themselves, they won't be able to serve their clients as well. In other words, your mantra is brilliant!"

Jeff nods his head. "I get the not apologizing . . . it's a muscle I'll continue to build. Fourth is potential, and its mantra is, humanity is hungry for your greatness. I believe we're all put on the planet to achieve great things. Imagine if we all realized our full potential. What a world this would be!"

"No doubt," Jessie responds. He gazes out and spies a set rolling in. "What's the final one?" he asks as he begins to turn his board.

"For autonomy," Jeff begins as he too turns his board, "ownership isn't automatic."

Amy has also turned her board, and the three surfers begin to paddle to set up for the first wave. Amy slots in in perfect position; Jessie and Jeff stop paddling and allow the wave to pass beneath them.

They begin paddling again for the second wave in the set. "Jeff, I absolutely love your mantras. Lean on them when things get rough. They'll get you through if you do." He begins to paddle alongside Jeff; this time, Jessie is in the best position. Jeff stops paddling and gives the wave to him.

As he paddles out a bit in anticipation of the next wave, he thinks, *Maybe that's it. All I have to do is lean into my mantras when things get tough and I'll stay on the path to reclaim my life.* He laughs and says out loud, "Sounds really simple, but it's probably not easy!" He catches a wave and floats down the face. At the bottom of the wave, he throws his hips in a deep right-hand turn, speeds up the face, and launches himself off the top into the air, giving an audible "whoop" as he flies. He splashes back down into the water, a huge grin on his face.

The three of them meet up again in the lineup. "Nice kick out, Jeff!" Amy says. You caught some good air."

"It felt awesome!" Jeff admits. "I think I've figured it out, Amy."

"Figured what out, Jeff?" she asks.

"I've figured out how to maintain my focus, momentum, and enthusiasm to reclaim my life."

"Jessie, you'll want to hear this." Amy waves him over. "Jeff was just telling me he's figured out how he'll maintain his momentum reclaiming his life."

"Love it, Jeff," Jessie says. "Whatcha got?"

"I know this will sound simple. I also know simple doesn't necessarily mean easy. I'm fighting a lot of momentum and current flowing in the opposite direction of me reclaiming my life."

Both Amy and Jessie nod in agreement.

"When things get tough, all I need to do is focus on my mantras. Have them at the ready, and keep the vision of what I want my life—" He pauses. "No that's not right, what I want my family's life to be."

"Awesome stuff, Jeff," Jessie says.

"That's great," Amy agrees.

"Well, it's time for me to head back in," Jessie says. "I've got a coaching call at the top of the hour and need to get my head right. Great seeing you, Amy, and great meeting you, Jeff!"

"I'll give you a call soon, Jessie," Amy says. "It's time we reengaged. I want to level up again and could use your guidance."

"You know where to find me," Jessie calls as he begins to turn his board. "Oh, and Jeff, have Amy give you my contact information. If and when you're ready, reach out. I'd love to coach you to help you realize your full potential and optimize your life." With that, he starts paddling back to shore.

They call out their goodbyes, and Jeff turns back to Amy. He's curious about her desire to start coaching sessions again.

Especially when she seems to have it all—at least mostly—figured out.

"Have you slipped back, Amy?" Jeff asks her. "Is that why you want to get Jessie to coach you again?"

"Nope, I wouldn't say that," Amy says. "It's more that even when you're at a high level, what got you there won't get you to the next one."

"Wait, there's more work for you to do?" Jeff asks, a bit flummoxed.

"There's always more work to do, Jeff," Amy replies. "Don't be overwhelmed by that. We take it one step at a time. You've got work to do reclaiming your life. So focus on doing that. You'll know when you're ready to level up from there . . . trust me."

They agree to ride one more wave. As they sit quietly waiting for the next set, Jeff says, "This coaching stuff really works, doesn't it?"

"What do you think, Jeff?"

"It's working for me, that's for sure."

"I remember one time you mentioned Bill Gates's TED talk where he said everyone needs a coach," Amy says. "Again, if that guy needs a coach and having one helped him reach his full potential, why not us?" She turns her board and prepares to catch her final wave of the session. "Hold that thought, Jeff, this one's mine!" She digs deeply as she paddles, pops up, and drops in.

Jeff waits for the next wave in the set and does the same. His ride shoreward is long and smooth. After the wave has lost its energy, he lays down and paddles smoothly, stands up and does the stingray shuffle onto the beach, where he reaches down and removes his leash and wraps it around the tail and fins of his board. Amy is there waiting for him, after having done the same thing.

"That was a great time," Amy says. "I do hope we get to do it again!"

"Same here, Amy. I had a blast surfing and talking. It was also great to meet Jessie. I like his vibe."

"Remind me to shoot you his contact information when we get back to the cars."

"Will do," Jeff says as he retrieves his bag. The two—lawyers, surfers, now friends—walk together toward the stairs. When they reach the shower on the stairs, each takes their turn. Then they make their way back up to the parking lot and begin to peel out of their wetsuits.

"So, Jeff, why do you think we lawyers tend to think we're different from C-suite executives, CEOs, or professional athletes when it comes to things like coaching?"

"Well, I think it probably comes down to our fine ability to bring together . . . ego and nonsense."

"That's a toxic mix," Amy chuckles.

"Indeed it is." Jeff giggles. "I'm so lucky you came over and introduced yourself that day, Amy. I never would have under-stood all this how I do now if you hadn't. I don't know how to thank you. I think I mentioned you opened Pandora's box with The 5 Lies, and you did—beautifully. But the truth of the matter is you've done so much more. Not only have I benefited from the work we've done together, but my firm and family have as well. It feels like everyone around me will eventually. I don't know how I could ever repay you."

Amy finishes tying her board to the roof rack. "Jeff, no thanks are necessary. Remember back when we first met I told you I wanted to reclaim the law as a noble profession?"

"I sure do," Jeff acknowledges. "That CLE seems like a lifetime ago."

Amy howls. "It certainly does. Anyway, you doing the work and reclaiming your life is thanks enough. The only other thing I would ask of you is when you see a lawyer struggling like you were, don't keep what you've learned a secret. Share it with them. Help them begin their journey."

"Will do."

"It's been a pleasure, Jeff! Be sure to keep in touch, because even if you don't, I know your assistant will speak with my assistant and I'll find out how you're doing anyway," she says playfully.

"I'll definitely keep in touch, and when you're up for another surf, just holler. If you give me enough lead time, I'll block out the morning. Next time we can hit Better Buzz afterward."

"You got it," Amy says and shares Jesse's cell number.

They shake hands, and as Jeff begins to pull away, Amy reaches out and hugs him. "You've done so well, Jeff." She steps back and looks him in the eye. "You've got this."

With that, she turns and gets into her car. As she begins to back away, she gives a final wave. Jeff waves back and gets into his car.

As he pulls out onto the highway, he feels relaxed and energized. *I've got this.* Then he speaks the words aloud. "I've really got this."

Jeff smiles. He's ready to continue doing the work of creating his own game and drafting his own rules. He's ready to fully reclaim his life.

Afterword

"The world doesn't need more conformists. The world needs more people who create and question and search."

~ LAIRD HAMILTON

Jeff's ongoing work isn't going to be easy; nothing worth doing typically is.

As lawyers, we have external obstacles like billable hour requirements, obligations, and societal expectations, to name a few. Add to that the internal obstacles, like GAILs—gremlins, assumptions, inferences, and limiting beliefs—and the blind spots we all have. There are so many ways to get off track and fall back into old habits. I know because it's happened to me.

The 5 Lies? My own journey is the basis for them. The five mantras, yes, those are mine as well. They are the result of more than twenty-four years as a practicing lawyer, twenty years as a litigator, sixteen years as a small law firm owner and leader, and a life spent exploring personal improvement and peak potential.

Here's the truth. I haven't always hit the mark on my focus. Also, I fully recognize I haven't walked one second in your shoes. I offer The Lies and mantras as concepts to consider and adopt for yourself or use as inspiration to create your own. These anchors became my way of keeping focused on moving forward, every damn day, no matter what, and I hope they offer you support as well. Additionally, I urge you to download and use the tools I've mentioned throughout this book by scanning the QR code you'll find on page 230. They are my gifts to you.

Whatever tools you utilize, the most crucial thing to do is hop off the hamster wheel, jump off the treadmill, insert your own clichéd visual here, and STOP. Look around. Ask yourself if you've got the life you thought you'd have before you crossed the threshold of law school the first time.

If the answer is yes, first ask yourself if that's really true. Then ask, were you thinking big enough?

If, on the other hand, the answer is no, ask yourself where you got lost.

My wish for you is nothing short of a reclaimed life; a life of independence, influence, and true wealth. A life that enriches your internal world with a sense of meaning, enhances your relationships and role as a leader, and ensures you are living the purpose you are intended to live in your time on earth. I also wish for you to identify and reach your full potential; we were all placed on this planet to do great things.

Knowledge without action is useless.

This book provides the knowledge, and now it is up to you to act.

As you do, I hope you remember: There's never a good reason to settle. It's weakness to allow others to define your success. Doing for others is honorable; doing for others and yourself is noble. Humanity is hungry for your greatness. Ownership isn't automatic.

Reclaiming your life is a journey. And now is the time to begin. Go. Do. Become.

About the Author

JOHN R. KORMANIK is a lawyer who coaches lawyers. He teams with outstanding attorneys around the world, empowering them to achieve their full potential through leadership and performance coaching. He holds a Professional Certified Coach designation from the International Coaching Federation. John has teamed up with in-house counsel in some of the most well-known organizations in the world, managing partners in mid-sized law firms, as well as with true solo lawyers who have an entrepreneurial mindset and ethos and want to achieve their full potential. Prior to pivoting to coaching, John practiced law for twenty-four years, owning and leading a successful small law firm for sixteen of them. John currently calls Boise, Idaho, home base, with his wife, Michelle, and his yellow Labrador retriever, Olive. His daughter, Allie, lives close by. Boise is considered "home base" because John has a passion for travel, which he does regularly, spending up to three months somewhere else in the world at any given time. You can visit his website at www.john rkormanik.com.

Complementary Resources

Throughout this book, I've shared resources provided by Amy to Jeff for his use in reclaiming his life. Because you have invested your most valuable asset—your time—in reading this book, I am happy to make those resources available to you at no charge.

By scanning the QR code below, you'll gain access to some of the tools used by Jeff. You'll also receive a foundational "Career Performance Assessment," which will empower you to rate your performance and satisfaction in eight specific areas of your career.

To unlock your complementary resources, simply scan the QR code with your mobile device. You'll be prompted to enter your name and email address. This will not only give you immediate access to invaluable resources but also ensure you receive ongoing updates and new resources as they become available.

http://www.breakthelawbook.com/resources

Reclaim *Your* Life

Continue the work of transforming your life and practice beyond *Break the Law*.

The author's insights do not end on the last page of this book. They come alive as you engage with them through various bespoke opportunities offered by John R. Kormanik Coaching:

- **1:1 Coaching:** Customized 1:1 leadership and performance coaching, creating a space where you can be authentic and empowered to reach your full potential.

- **Leadership Workshops:** Tailored sessions that focus on cultivating leadership qualities in law firm partners to drive firm success in a sustainable way.

- **Keynote Speaking:** Live speaking engagements to ignite a passion for innovative leadership and high performance among attendees at your next Continuing Legal Education event or conference.

Seize the opportunity to revolutionize both the mindset and the metrics of your legal practice. Engage with John R. Kormanik to bring these powerful narratives to life for you, in your firm, or upcoming event, ensuring a future where your firm doesn't merely participate in the market, but leads it.

Contact us at **john@johnrkormanik.com**.